SOMETHING FOR YOU FROM SUNDERLAND

Old Sunderland as portrayed in the postcards
of the Billy Dent Collection.

Compiled and edited by Stuart Miller
and the members of the Monkwearmouth Local History Group

Dedicated to

Ella Dent

First published 1997

Copyright © Stuart Miller and Billy Dent 1997

The People's History
Suite 1
Byron House
Seaham
Co. Durham
SR7 0PW

ISBN 1 899560 44 0

Contents

SOMETHING FOR YOU FROM SUNDERLAND

Within this postman's bag you'll find
An interesting gift consigned.

Regd. No. 569868

834

Something for you from Sunderland

This was a fairly standard postcard which seems to have been 'customised' for use in a number of places, e.g. "Something for you from Bournemouth". The message is sent from Elsinore House in Cleadon and dated 12 July 1914. It is addressed to Miss Mary Ericksen. "My dear little Mary. How are you keeping? Do you like to be in London. We miss you very much dear. Well Mary you are to miss all of the strawberries in the garden and they are nice, you must come and get some when you get back. Mage sends you a nice kiss she wants you to play with her when you come home. Goodnight little girl & may God bless & keep you from all harm. From your Aunty Sarah. XXXXX"

INTRODUCTION

The purpose of this book is to give the reader a glimpse of Sunderland in the earlier years of the 20th Century. The medium adopted for this excursion into the past is a series of postcards. The area covered geographically is the main area of the borough, and outlying districts have not been covered. The reason for this selectivity has not been for any other reason than that the postcards used are derived from a personal collection which has been accumulated over the years and the emphasis of that collection has been on the districts which are included. Our apologies are due to the folk of the neglected areas of which postcards do exist and may well be included in other publications and collections.

On the whole the postcards which have been preferred are from the period before 1939, many of them before the First World War. Postcards more recent than the 1950s do figure in the collection but we agreed generally to ignore them so that a greater chronological focus could be achieved and because they were, frankly, less interesting. The dating of the scenes and postcards was one of the many trials and tribulations involved in assembling the book for publication, and we may have often got it wrong. Wherever the date has been guessed we have suggested the evidence upon which the conjecture is based.

I have talked about 'we'. One of the other major features of this book is that considerable reliance has been placed upon information and anecdotes provided by the members of the Monkwearmouth Local History Group. Together with the other history groups and societies of the town the Monkwearmouth Local History Group has done much to retrieve and make available old photographs of Sunderland and also oral reminiscences of life and work within it. This is a book which has grown from the community.

The other 'contributors' have been the authors of the postcards themselves. One of the most pleasurable aspects of working with postcards is the opportunity it gives, at least to someone as naturally inquisitive as me, to eavesdrop and to pry into the lives of other people through the medium of their scribbled messages to friends, family and colleagues. Of course the authors or recipients of some of the more recent cards may still, hopefully, be very much alive and well so we apologise for quoting from their private jottings. If anyone does recognise any of these messages we would be very glad to hear from them. On the whole the printed versions of the messages relate as closely as possible to the original written versions so as to maintain the personal tone. However where the writers clearly intended that grammatical dictates should be followed but were simply the victims of haste I have helpfully inserted the occasional full-stop! One of the postcards was written in Italian, one in Russian, one in Swedish and one in standard shorthand and translations of these are provided.

As well as the messages attached to them each of the scenes has a brief commentary which has been put together with the help of the members of the Monkwearmouth Local History Group and Messrs. Billy Dent and Alan Brett. If there are errors I will hastily attribute them to my colleagues who are, after all, mostly senior to myself in years and therefore in a position to know better! Again we would welcome from readers any comments as to accuracy or amplification of the information.

My role in all this has been that of the professional historian: to structure the contents, to describe the broader historical context, to question the information provided and to edit vigorously.

Postcards

The first plain message postcard was introduced in the Habsburg Monarchy in 1869. The first British cards were on sale in October 1870 bearing, at a $^1/2$d, half the current letter rate of postage. The development of picture postcards was delayed by the charging of the full letter rate until 1894 for anything other than the dull, officially printed cards, and by the requirement until 1902 that the whole of one side must bear both the stamp and the addressee's name and address. After 1902 the floodgates were opened to the new divided back, picture postcard.

Most of the postcards represented in this book are what are called topographicals. That is to say they are general views of beaches, piers and promenades, urban streets and so on. For the early 20th Century topographical photographer the best time to work was in the early morning when there was time to set up the cumbersome apparatus and the inconvenience of thronging, curious and staring multitudes could be evaded. In fact most of these views are full of vitality. Cards without people and activity were, well, discarded. A number of them are the products of prominent British publishers of photographic views, such as Lilywhite Ltd and Valentine and Sons of Dundee. Some of them clearly bear the mark of local photographers such as Auty and Hastings who covered most of County Durham and the Tyne-Wear region. The Newcastle Central Library holds an excellent archive of their work.

Of course there are many other types of card and examples of most of them are included here. The comic postcard was on the scene very soon. There are a few good seaside examples in this collection. The most famous comic artist was Donald McGill (1875-1962) who populated his world with buxom women, cheeky children and hen-pecked husbands. Those included here are quite modest compared to some of the risque products of the genre. Companies and tradespeople had latched on to the advertising value of postcards from the beginning, especially at half the postage price. A couple of examples are included here, one of them bearing a brief business message to a fellow tradesman. Then there are the special commemoratives produced to signal some special event or occasion. In fact this was as likely to extend to accidents and mishaps as well as to exhibitions, shows and royal visits. Sometimes these souvenirs bore a commemorative postmark as well.

All of these types of postcard and other styles were given a huge boost by the First World War. Topographical, humorous, sentimental and commemorative cards flowed in torrents between members of the armed services and their sweethearts, families and friends. A couple of the cards herein are from soldiers to their girlfriends or mothers during the First World War, one of them apparently on his way to the climactic fighting of 1917-18. In fact soldiers preferred two styles of postcard, sketches of under-dressed young women for themselves and sentimental or patriotic silk embroidered cards for their wives and sweethearts. Certain standards do need to be observed after all!

If you are interested in looking into the subject of picture postcards and collecting them there is a brief bibliography at the back of this book. You would do well to start with the little booklet *Picture Postcards* by C. W. Hill (Shire, 1987) though.

We do hope you enjoy this 'Something for you from Sunderland'.

Stuart Miller

Monkwearmouth Library

This card is addressed to Mrs. Dun, Mount Pleasant, California, Great Ayton, Yorkshire. The date is 29 September, 1918.

"Dear Sister. I received P.C. alright and I will meet that train on Saturday morning. The boy was proud of his cards. He did chatter when there was one from Granda. He is busy writing to him this morning as soon as he gets a bit of paper and pencils. He is writing to Granda. We are having grand weather here if only it keeps like it for a bit. Love to all, Alice."

Indeed Monkwearmouth Library has changed little if at all. Much of the initial work in producing this book was done in the library so it deserves to be included. It is also the meeting place for the Monkwearmouth Local History Group.

Acknowledgements

My thanks are due especially to:

Billy Dent, whose collection forms the basis of this book.

Susan Dent for her help in translating near-illegible messages.

Bob Robinson for much of the text for the River Section.

Archie Donaldson, Frank Dembry and the members of the Monkwearmouth Local History Group for their help in identifying details in many of the pictures.

Frank Charlton for his knowledgeable assistance regarding the tramways.

Dennis Bulmer for his comments about the Roker and Seaburn postcards.

Elsie Ronald for translating a postcard message in shorthand.

Frank Beardow for translating the Russian postcard message.

Shelagh and Finn Orbeck for translating the Swedish postcard message.

Alan Brett for his constant friendship, and Black Cat Publications for undertaking the difficult task of publishing this book.

The ever helpful, good natured and coffee supplying staff of Monkwearmouth Branch Library

SECTION ONE

THE RIVER AND THE DOCKS

Quite rightly our postcard illustrated journey around Sunderland starts with the river which has always been at the heart of the development and growth of the town. Until relatively recently most of the major industries of Sunderland were linked to the river in some way. Having said that if someone in the past had been faced with the need to make a conscious decision regarding the siting of Sunderland they may well have not chosen the Wear! It took the River Wear Commissioners, established in 1717, to adapt the river to the needs of a rapidly growing town and its diversity of industries.

On the River
"Dear Willie. Arrived all safe & sound 3.50. Mrs. Taylorson came to meet me but we missed on the way. The children are splendid. Will write a letter the first oppo. Kind love from all to all. Nellie." The card is addressed to Master Wm. Barr, Auriel House, Gt. Broughton, Stokesley, Yorkshire.

The River Wear

This is a view of the Wear west of the Wearmouth Bridge showing on the left the coal staiths of the Lambton and Hetton Collieries. The distinctive bands (red on black) of the Lambton and Hetton tug-boats and collier can be seen. In the far distance is the Deptford works of Sir James Laings shipyard. To the right of the picture are the staiths and structure of Wearmouth Colliery and the Wreath Quay

Sunderland from the Bridge

The post mark is 30 May, 1906. The card was posted in Boston, Massachusetts. The view is of the Wear from Wearmouth Bridge. To the right is S.P. Austins. Just in view at the bottom right side is the stern of a vessel on the Pontoon. The graving dry dock just beyond the small vessel is empty. In the far background is the old Sunderland quayside. To the right of the picture are two Lambton and Hetton paddle tugs. Beyond is a distinctive William Doxford and Sons turret ship. The first one was built in 1893. The last one was built in 1911. There were 178 in total.

W. Parry.

LAUNCH OF S.S. "WHATELEY HALL," June 16th, 1904,
THE 100TH TURRET STEAMER,
WILLIAM DOXFORD & SONS, LTD., SHIPBUILDERS AND ENGINEERS.
PALLION YARD, SUNDERLAND.

Launch of S.S. Whateley Hall, June 16th, 1904. The 100th Turret Steamer, William Doxford and Sons Ltd., Shipbuilders and Engineers. Pallion Yard, Sunderland.

A long but precise title. The message seems to read as follows:
"The dog biscuits you sent off Aug 19th must be at Blakny (Blakeney?) by this time. Make inquiries from the owner." It is addressed to Mr. Alex Pringle, Gamekeeper, Elm House, Farndale, Kirbymoorside. There is not a clear signature or initial, but it is written in a very authoritative tone!

The River

"Thank you so much for your nice letter. Auntie F. and I had tea with Matron today. Love and kisses. Mother" (the address is illegible)

River Wear from Bridge

The Pontoon

This is a general view of the Wear taken from the Wearmouth Bridge. It shows at the centre right the S.P. Austin Pontoon (opened in 1903) and beyond that is the graving dry dock which was opened in 1870 on the site of a previous repair slipway. The dock could accommodate vessels of up to 300 feet in length. Further back still can be seen the shipbuilding berths of S.P. Austin which opened on this site in 1846. To the left are vessels lying at John Dickinson and Sons, Engineering Co. which was established in 1852. In the background are vessels being fitted out at J.L. Thompsons Manor Quay Works. The picture may date to the mid-1930s when shipbuilding was beginning to pick up again on the basis of the government's Scrap and Build Scheme.

The Pontoon Dock, River Wear.

Sunderland.

Hills, Sunderland.

The Pontoon Dock

The card is addressed to Mr. Cleminson, School House, Bothel, Aspatria, Carlisle. It reads: "Yours to hand. Hope you enjoyed your holidays. Had Mr. Lewis H.M.I. for company. Says he was at Westminster College when you were. Wishes to be remembered to you. Got settled again. Hope you have a successful treat. Yrs. B.E.C."

The date is 21 August, 1906.

S.P. Austin Shipbuilders and Ship Repairers were based at the Wear Dockyard, Panns Bank. The firm was started by Peter Austin on the north side of the river at North Sands in 1826. It moved to the south bank in 1846. The 'Pontoon' or Floating Dock was opened and commissioned in 1903 on the site of the bottleworks which previously occupied the riverside there. The site was purchased in 1897. The first vessel docked here was the Cunard Line S.S. *Brescia*. The Pontoon was capable of taking vessels of up to 400 feet in length and was a tremendous asset to the company. It was constructed in two sections to enable maintenance to be carried out by placing one section onto the other for underwater cleaning and painting. There was an inside wall with side supports and adjustable blocks to carry the current vessel under repair at keel and bilge positions. The Pontoon was submerged and refloated using a ballast and water tank system. S.P. Austin closed in 1967. The Pontoon was taken off to Rotterdam to be scrapped.

Flotilla visit to Sunderland, 1904

This would be one of the many passenger ferries taking people beyond the piers to view the Naval Flotilla in 1904. The photograph seems to have been taken inside the South Docks entrance. This would have been in serious trouble nowadays because of the lack of provision for safety. Apart from the occasional lifebuoy ring there is no obvious provision. The passengers would have been seated on wooden seats on an open deck. The steering wheel is situated in the aft well of the vessel. At least the seats might have acted as safety rafts in the event of an accident. Brave souls! This year saw the record export of coal from Sunderland, with an amazing total of 5,117,230 tons. From then on the total began to fall and with them the income of the River Wear Commissioners and the coal receipts of the NER. This explains partly why the RWC ceased work on the new South Pier. Paradoxically (but typically it would be claimed by cynical observers of the spending of money by private and public bodies...) this was the very time when the RWC and NER chose to ensconce themselves in newer offices which were more in keeping with their status. The RWC moved to their grand building at the corner of St. Thomas Street and John Street and the NER took up residence in new offices built at Burdon House.

On the Wear at Sunderland
A general view of vessels in the Wear around 1910. There is a mixture of sail and steam.
The vessels raising their sails are adjacent to the present Fish Quay. In the background is
the recently restored Rose Line Building at Wylam Wharf. To the right can be seen a vessel
lying at Manor Quay. Beyond can be seen Austin's Shipyard and the Wearmouth Bridge.

Wm. France, Fenwick and Co. Ltd., Sunderland
The vessel is the *King John*. She was launched from the North Sands on the 18 August, 1906
by J.L. Thompson and Son. She was registered at Stockton. She was 6,071 tons and
belonged to the King Line Ltd. The paddle tug-boat was the *Marsden*. She was built in 1906
and belonged to France-Fenwick and Co. Ltd. of Sunderland. In 1921 she was sold to the
British Tug Company and renamed *Mumbles*. The tug-boat was involved in the
Dardanelles Campaign in the First World War. She was wrecked at Suvla Bay.

HMS Cyclops

The card is addressed to Miss Christie, 135 Portman St., Middlesbrough. It seems to be dated 1907.

"This is a view of the ship that is now on show in the dock. Father has been acting as an official to day & is going to do so next Sat, so I think we will wait till then. If Miss Maughan would like this view you can give it to her as we have other two, Father bought them on the ship. We expect you Mon. Jennie."

Sir James Laings got into financial difficulties in converting the vessel into a naval repair ship. Their loss was estimated at £100,000, a lot of money in 1907! H.M.S *Cyclops* was built originally for T.B. Roydens of Liverpool in 1905. The picture shows the Lifeboat Station in the background situated at the North Dock entrance (to the left of the tug-boat funnel). The paddle tug was probably owned by James Ridley Steam Tug Co. and may have been the *Wonder*. The insignia was a blue star and a black band on a white funnel. There is a gun on the fore deck of *Cyclops*. You can see clearly the rivetted seams on the shell of the vessel. There is an open wheelhouse and navigation bridge. There is a small foyboat coble at the side of the ship. She may be going in to the Dry Dock at Greenwells.

The Docks, Sunderland

The Docks

The date is 10 April, 1915. The message is addressed to a Miss Thirwell, Seaham Hall, By Sunderland, Durham.

"Dear M. I arrived quite safe about 10 o'clock. 2 hours late getting to Kings Cross. Train went wrong road. Everything here looks lovely. Hope all are well. Will write. E.M."

The picture is a nice combination of sail and steam. It is a view of Sunderland Docks showing the Coal Staiths behind at the left side. One of the sailing vessels bears the Norwegian flag. It is reassuring to find that even in those days the railway system was fallible, and going by the 'wrong road' is far more imaginative than damp autumn leaves on the rails.

The Channel Fleet off Roker

The card is addressed to a Miss S.G. at Wool Knoll, Hovingham, Near York. This is an Auty-Hastings card. You have to wonder about the human relationships here. Would you send a girlfriend a photo of the Channel Fleet? The North Breakwater was complete by then. What really makes this photograph is the squadrons of bathing huts on the beach.

The South Outlet and Fish Quay. *Hope to see you soon let me know when you are coming over. Tell me in good time so I can arrange to meet you.* Sunderland.

The South Outlet and Fish Quay
This card is addressed to Miss J. Taylor, 33 Hurworth Terrace, Neasham Road, Darlington.
"3.11.5
<u>My Dear</u> Old Jen. Just a line to let you know I started my new crib yesterday & up till now have done <u>excedenly well</u>. I don't feel quite up to the mark yet as far as health is concerned but after what I done, it has gone a long way towards making me feel much better. <u>I know you will feel pleased to hear this news</u>. I have had two houses from that man, but they were rather large for us. 6 & 5 rooms & rather heavy rents. <u>I hope before long</u> he will manage to get us one. <u>I hope you are feeling better</u> & that I will see you soon. I will write you tomorrow & let you know all. I am going out with our manager on business tonight or I should have written you a letter. Yours Ted."

The Open Lifeboat is being launched at the South Lifeboat Station into the Hendon Channel with full crew on board. The Lifeboat was probably steered by side oars and a stern helmsman. Two paddle tugs are shown at the then Fish Quay in the Hendon Channel. The Channel had direct access to the North Sea from the Hudson Dock South Sea Lock and from the Hendon Dock. At this time, I believe, Sunderland Port was served by two lifeboats, one south and one at or near the old inner North Pier. The lifeboats were kept very busy by the many sailing ships entering the port in bad weather.

SECTION TWO

BRIDGES, FERRIES AND TRAMS

In fact the River Wear has been more of an obstacle than an aid to the development of Sunderland. This is true of it in the sense that it had to be adapted to the needs of shipping and shipbuilding and also because it was an obstacle to regional land communications for many years. Sunderland has a respectable status in the history of bridge building. Nevertheless ferries continued to play a part in the local Wearside communications network until the 1950s. Also of great significance in the development of Sunderland was the tramways system. Here we encounter for the first time those 'swaying galleons of delight' which will reappear constantly in this book.

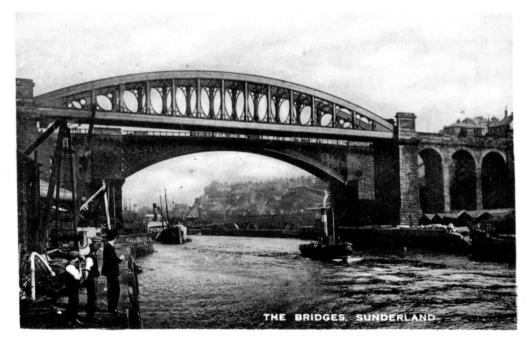

The Bridges
Viewed from upstream from the north side.

The Bridges
This card is addressed to Rif. E. Smith, 6766 E. Coy., 1st B.B., Palace Bks., Belfast. It seems to be dated 1907.
"Dear Smirks. I send you this hoping you will receive it alright. I arrived safe and well hoping you did the same ... are you allowed out yet. I got drunk on Saturday and had a decent drink last night. Give my best respects to all the coy. Jim."
This is a superb photograph which bears all of the hallmarks of Auty-Hastings of Newcastle. The original Wearmouth Bridge, sponsored and at least in part designed by the banker Rowland Burdon, had been opened in 1796. It was not, in truth, very robust and had to be greatly strengthened in 1805 lest it fell down. Then in 1857-59 it was totally rebuilt by Robert Stephenson. The ribs of the original bridge remained, albeit disguised by the insertion of new wrought iron arches. The abutments were raised as well so that the distinctive hump of the original bridge was eliminated. Stephenson's bridge was joined by the railway bridge in 1879. Until then there were two separate railway networks on either side of the river. In 1879 the NER closed the gap and linked Monkwearmouth with Ryhope Grange. The bridge was designed by Thomas Harrison. In its day it was the largest single arched hog backed iron girder bridge in the world.

A postcard with exactly the same scene was also sent overseas.

The Bridges
The message written on this card is in Swedish. It is addressed to a Master Hakon Kohler, Borringe Tegelbruk, Borringe, Skane, Sweden. It is dated 17 August, 1907.
"Dear Hakon! I'm sending you the warmest wishes for your birthday and wish you all the very best for the coming year! I am now staying with the Gregerssons with 'Sid' and have been here since last Saturday and will stay until one day next week. Having a very enjoyable time as there are so many new people to meet. I am waiting <u>so much</u> for a letter from Mamma! Hope you are all well. My very best wishes to you dear little Hakon, Mother, Father, Elsa-Greten and the Westergards from all of us, sent by Aunt Hildurh (you know who!). P.S. Ask Mamma to write to me soon!"

The Bridges

The card is addressed to Mrs. A. Gibbon, 109 Ewart Road, Forest Fields, Nottingham. It is dated 20 June (or July), 1916.

"Dear M. I am just writing this postcard to let you know that I have just received the welcome registered letter this afternoon Tuesday after coming back from Sunderland baths. Warm this time not cold shower. But that means you should not have bothered sending that positive order as you can do with all you can get from the main office. I'll try to manage the best I can but many thank yous for it and that other parcel. Yours affectionate. Albert."

Confusing isn't it ?

Bridges and the River Wear

This view is from upstream of the bridges from the south side of the river.

Sunderland Bridge and Lambton Coal Drops
A very similar postcard has the message:
"Thanks for your card. I hope you will like this. Love from Lottie." This is addressed to
Miss L. Rattcliff, Newtown Farm, Cross Green, nr. Shrewsbury.

The building of the new Wearmouth Bridge
"This is the New Bridge at Sunderland which the Prince of Wales opened."
Stephenson's bridge survived until the 1920s. The present Wearmouth Bridge was erected
around the old one so that traffic movement was not interrupted. The ribs of Burdon's
bridge disappeared at this time and not even one example of a voissoir block was retained
although some of the iron work of the church at Castle Eden is said to be from the original
bridge.

The Duke of York opens
new Wearmouth Bridge

The Duke of York opens the new Wearmouth Bridge
The big day arrives. There is a smart guard of honour. The white stand is there to allow
access to the point on the bridge where the famous silver rivet is being placed. There
appear to be people right up on the lower transverse girders of the bridge.

THE NEW BRIDGE, SUNDERLAND.

The New Bridge
The present Wearmouth Bridge was designed by Mott, Hay, and Anderson and was built
around the old one so as to keep traffic moving. It was constructed in 1927-29 and opened
in 1929 by the Duke of York, the future King George VI. The ceremonial silver rivet was the
last to be inserted. It is actually quite a fine bridge in its own right although it cannot aspire
to be a record breaker or record holder in any respect.

WEAR BRIDGE. SUNDERLAND.

Wear Bridge
There is no message and no date. The position of the silver rivet seems to be marked.

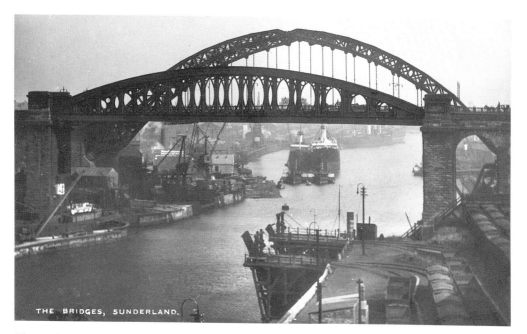

The Bridges

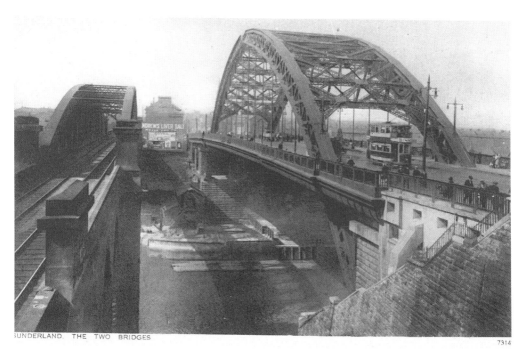

The Two Bridges

48. Sunderland: Queen Alexandra Bridge.

Queen Alexandra Bridge

The message on this card is expressed in shorthand. It reads as follows: "Dear Joe. I hope you enjoyed the final part of your holidays very nicely. Congratulations on the photoes (sic). I am sorry to say that up to now I have been presented in Sunderland with nothing but wet weather but today seems to promise well. But at the same time I have been enjoying myself pretty well <u>you know</u>. I hope work is not so heavy as when I left it. Goodbye. Will. Many thanks for your card Joe. This is the largest bridge over the River Wear at the mouth of which stands my native town." The card is dated 25 June, 1913 and addressed to Belgrave Road, London. It is not clear what the '<u>you know</u>' refers to! Will seems to have found some source of underlined delight in Sunderland.

THE ALEXANDRA BRIDGE, SUNDERLAND.

The Alexandra Bridge

The bridge was the subject of many postcards. It was then known as The New Wear Bridge. Only on the occasion of its opening on the 10 June, 1909 by the Earl of Durham was it revealed that the Queen had given permission for it to be named after her. The 2,600 ton centre span of this massive two level road and rail bridge was the heaviest in Britain. The monster was designed by Charles A. Harrison for the LNER and Sunderland Corporation and was constructed by Sir William Arrol and Co. Ltd. The contract price was £325,000 of which the Corporation agreed to pay £146,000 because of the road deck. In fact the estimates were exceeded (surprise, surprise!) and the Corporation was landed with a bill for about £200,000 towards the total of £450,000. Designed to carry coal trains from west Durham to the South Dock it was always somewhat of a white elephant because by the time it was opened the trade was already in decline. In fact until the early 1920s there was only one regular coal train a week and then rail traffic ceased entirely.

Queen Alexandra Bridge

This card is addressed to Mr. and Mrs. F. Birtwhistle, 95 Surrey Street, Middlesbrough. It is dated 22 August, 1910.

"Dear Friends. I just want you to have a look at the Sunderland New Bridge. The Weight of the river span is 2,600 tons and length 420 feet. Observe new 100 ton crane alongside. That is the Southwick Engine Works where I worked last. I send kind regards. Your old friend Hubt. Clark."

Queen Alexandra Bridge

An odd legend associated with the bridge is that it was never fully utilised because there were faults in its construction. It is claimed that to save costs not all of the bolts were put in place. In fact the legend is right, but not about this bridge. It was the Tay Bridge, the central sections of which fell in December 1879, which was weakened by the excessive use of a filler substance called Beaumonts Egg made of beeswax, resin, iron borings and lamp black to fill cracks in faulty castings and bolt holes. A sort of home-made Polyfilla!

Wear Water Cottage, Hylton
This card is addressed to Mr. J. Lyons, Crois Pharmacy, Souterville, New York, USA.
"16 June 1913. Got your pipe, looks all right. But don't know how I will smoke, kind regards to Mrs. L. Got surely settled now? Yours etc. J. Chester."
It sounds as if Mr. Chester's jaw was wired up or something!

Below: The Ferry, Hylton
This card is addressed to Miss A. Jenkins, 28 Portland Place, Stevenson, Ayrshire, Scotland.
"Dear Annie. We arrived home safe about 2 o'clock on Sunday morning, thank you for your company I enjoyed it very much, my face is better it is alright since the babbie has seen it."
The ferry between North and South Hylton dated back to at least the 17th Century, and probably was in existence from medieval times. It was painted by the famous northern artist Ralph Hedley (1910). There was a chain operated ferry for vehicles and a rowing boat for passengers. The latter continued until 1957.

WEAR WATER COTTAGE, HYLTON.   S.A.C.   Nº 4.

THE FERRY, HYLTON.   Nº 5.

Penshaw Monument

Admittedly neither a bridge nor a ferry but having come so far up the river we may as well glance at the greatest landmark in County Durham.

It is said of Sunderland that it is the only place in the world where you can stand by a mock Greek temple and look down on a mock Roman bridge. This seems to be a pre-First World War postcard judging from the length of the dresses of the women who must have cursed them under their breath as they laboured their way up the hill. The architects were John and Benjamin Green. The foundation stone of the monument was laid on 28 August, 1844. It was erected in memory of John George Lambton, the 1st Earl of Durham, who died in 1840. He was a leader of the campaign for parliamentary reform which resulted in the Great Reform Act of 1832, and was the author of the Durham Report on Canada which is regarded as the foundation document of the Commonwealth of Nations.

Penshaw Monument.

Hills Sunderland

It cost £3,000 to build, the money being raised by private subscription. The monument is made of gritstone mined from the Marsden quarry of the Marquis of Londonderry. It was modelled on the Theseion at Athens but is 100 feet long by 53 feet wide compared to the Greek version which is four feet longer and eight feet narrower. The Theseion has 54 columns, each 3 feet 4 inches thick while Penshaw has 18 which are twice as thick. The idea that the one is a replica of the other, therefore, should be regarded with suspicion! There is a staircase within one of the columns which leads to a walkway around the top. This was closed to the public from 1926 when a 16-year-old Fatfield apprentice mason called Temperly Scott fell to his death. There was a plaque on the monument but that has long ago disappeared. The text referred to the 'Distinguished Talents and Exemplary Private Virtues' of the Earl. No doubt those remarks are true, but he was also regarded with great suspicion and dislike by fellow politicians because of his assiduous self publicity. He was very much a man of our time of whom, it was said, that he had the text of his speeches in to the hands of the press before he made them.

Sunderland

This card is addressed to Miss E. Mill in Leith, Edinburgh.

"Dear Elise. I will be home on Saturday & my sister is coming through with me. The train leaves here at 6.21 am, so look out for me. This is all I have time to say as I am going to look for the comet so ta ta for the present from your loving chum S.E.L."

The comet referred to will have been Halley's Comet so that would date the card to 1910. A word or two about trams will be appropriate at this point.

From 1879 the Sunderland Tramways Company was running horse-drawn trams under lease from the Sunderland Corporation ('primitive vehicles lit by smoking oil lamps and with floors covered with straw in winter') from Roker via Fawcett Street, Christ Church, Gray Road and Tatham Street and back. Other lines were added in the later years of the century but served middle class areas pre-eminently. In 1900 the Council (following a 'freebie' visit by eight councillors and officers to Paris, Brussels and Hamburg ...) took over the tramways and began to electrify the system and extend it. The first electric tram ran between Christ Church and Roker on 15 August, 1900. The whole existing system was electrified by February, 1901 and the horses were out of a job. The system was extended to create a circular route via Hylton Road, Chester Road and Kayll Road and to link up to Grangetown and Sea Lane and Villette Road and there were added a new line from Roker Avenue to Fulwell (1903) and a branch to the Docks via Hudson Road (1904). The Corporation electric tram system was cheap. From 1900 to 1948 passengers could travel to any part of the system for 1d (or 0.4p for those readers who have forgotten the days of proper money). You had to sit on wooden benches though! And since these were longitudinal in the lower compartment you had to sit facing the person opposite with all of the awful eye contact implications! The downstairs compartment was reserved for non-smokers, while the wheezers and coughers could make their way upstairs.

Here can be seen two pre-1914 open topped double deck tramcars. Both seem to be on their way to Fulwell. In 1900-1902 the Corporation purchased 50 open topped double deck trams and 14 single deck trams. From 1904 onwards the open top trams were progressively rebuilt with open ended balcony top covers or totally enclosed. The Nestles Milk advert was positioned at the end of the bridge for many years and was a good eyecatcher. Just next to it was the Trustees Savings Bank. We shall continue our journey by tram into the main thoroughfares of the town.

Bridges

What seems to be tramcar No. 64 is crossing the Wearmouth Bridge towards the town centre. This is one of the open topped four wheel cars supplied by Dick, Kerr and Co. in 1902. These were all rebuilt as totally enclosed cars in later years. No. 64 was only rebuilt as late as 1933. Thankfully the seats on the upper decks of these open cars were wire woven 'Never Wet' seats, a patented type designed specially for wet weather.

Bridges

This is addressed to Edgar Byrnes, esq. 12, Eastlake Road, Camberwell, SE5. The date may be 1939 (the stamp is of that period). It could be an old postcard sent under a more recent stamp.

"Dear Jim, I thought you would be interested in the photo overleaf. It is a real old timer. I am getting copies of a postcard circulating in Croydon showing one of the old trams in the middle of the town. Can you give me Gill Knight's address. I want to get her along on Friday, Dec. 30th if possible? Ronald."

So postcard collecting is clearly a well established hobby. It is to be hoped that Ronald had some luck with Gill Knight.

FAWCETT STREET AND BRIDGE STREET

Emerging from the riverside we must move on to Bridge Street and Fawcett Street which is the main thoroughfare of the city although it has been rather schizophrenic since the development of the Bridges shopping centre which contributed to the reduction of the commercial significance of Fawcett Street. Of course as with many towns there have been frequent changes in the commercial axis. Before the Fawcett Street - Bridge Street axis developed in the mid-19th Century it was High Street and Low Street which were the key to the commercial and cultural life of the town and at the time when most of these photographs were taken they were still very busy and important streets.

High Street

A view down High Street with the Havelock on the right and Mackie's Corner on the left. A rather apprehensive (...please rescue me from this woman ...) boy with a very thin lipped (...just wait till I get you home my boy ...) mother is just about to cross from right to left. Manfield and Sons are advertising boots under 'The Sign of Quality' as 'Worn All Over The World' (...a little ambiguously perhaps). It's amazing how often these postcards and photographs have passing policemen in them. It's as if they had nothing better to do than lurk around until the button was being pressed, then sweep officiously across.

Borough Road
"This is one of the main streets in Sunderland. Love Ezra."
This card, with its curt message, is dated June, 1924 and addressed to Mr. Horner, 38 Craig Street, Darlington.

Thoughts of You from Sunderland
It is addressed to a Miss Miller in Morpeth. There is no clear date. It looks pre-1914. The message reads:
"My Dear Daughter. I was glad to get your letter and so very pleased you felt a little better. I hope you will feel alright again when you come back. We have had bad weather since you went away and it is still very cold, there was a white frost this morning. Father is still keeping a lot better. Tom is still not working. Lots of love from your loving Mother."

Fawcett Street
A view of Fawcett Street from Burdon Road beside the park.

Fawcett Street
Binns Drapers can be seen next to Webster and Shewans. In its remorseless creep along Fawcett Street it would swallow up its neighbour. S.S. Eades rather imposing shop front can be seen on the other side of Fawcett Street. It would go bankrupt and be taken over by C.J. Vincents. Two trams can be seen. In front is an open topped double decker en route to the docks. Behind it is a closed top double decker. The docks tramline was the first one to be removed in 1928 when the route was taken over by buses

Fawcett Street

The Fawcett Street development was based on land which had belonged to the wealthy Fawcett family of Newcastle. When the bridge was built in 1796 a natural consequence was that the axis of the town began to swing to the North-South line. A few sets of cunningly positioned traffic lights can have the same effect nowadays! From about 1820 the streets were planned and building leases were sold. By 1850 an estate of terraces had been created. As well as Fawcett Street there were also the streets which run parallel to it although they were developed rather later. They take their names also from the Fawcett family - John Street, Frederick Street, Foyle Street.

On the corner opposite to the Town Hall stood the Athenaeum. It was opened in 1841 and was the home of the Literary and Philosophical Society. It contained a lecture room and library and was the home of the antiquarian collections which were the foundation for the museum. It housed the museum from 1840 and the library from 1868. In 1859 the bailiffs were called in and the Literary and Philosophical Society was closed. The Athenaeum then became the Liberal Club. It was fronted by classical Greek columns in the Ionic style. These were removed before 1910 because they were an obstruction. They do not seem to be present at the time of this photograph. The site is now occupied by the Electricity Showrooms and the Athenaeum Buildings. The electrification of the tramways system from 1900 is an aid in dating pictures, at least in very general terms.

The boy to the right of the woman in the foreground has no shoes. He seems to be carrying a bundle of washing or some such thing on his head. The two policemen seem very conscious of the presence of the camera.

Fawcett Street

The site of the late and lamented old Town Hall was selected only after a considerable debate about the merits of rivals including the Grange, Sunniside and the site of the Mowbray Park Hotel. In 1883 the land in Fawcett Street was purchased but it was only in 1886 that it was agreed to organise a competition with three prizes for the design of the building. Brightwen Binyon was the successful architect and the foundation stone was laid on 9 September, 1887. The Town Hall was completed in three years at a cost of £48,000 as compared to the original estimate of £30,000. Its opening was the subject of a procession, musical entertainment, a fireworks display and a gargantuan banquet for the civic party. In fact it was too small for its purpose within ten years and various departments had to be housed in other accommodation. There were plans drawn up for its extension in 1903 but these were never carried through. Its demolition caused considerable controversy, and that might be seen as a factor in producing a more sensitive policy towards the historic buildings of Sunderland.

Here can be seen Binns Drapers, Furriers and (probably) Furniture. Next to Binns is Webster and Shewans, Furriers.

Fawcett Street.   Sunderland.

Hills—Sunderland.

Fawcett Street

The clock of the Town Hall had a special place in the hearts of Wearsiders. It was installed by William Potts and Sons of Leeds. It was known as a Cambridge Quarter. Five bells formed the Westminster Chimes. They were cast by John Warner and Sons of Cripplegate, London who also cast Big Ben. Every New Year there was the ritual of runners, perhaps not entirely sober, trying to sprint the length of Fawcett Street within the twelve chimes. There was a storm of protest at the demise of the clock, and the special clock tower promised by the Council in compensation was never built. When the Bridges complex was built the working mechanism of the clock was put on display in a transparent case as if to taunt the passing citizens! The bells could not be used in such a confined space so a synchronised recording of the bells of Durham Cathedral had to be used instead. In fact in 1983 four of them were stolen from the Civic Centre car park anyhow. The old clock faces had corroded beyond redemption so three-foot wide copies were installed instead. Rather a sad story!

The street is alive with the sound of tramcars. In the lead is the open topped double decked No. 1 tramcar. This was one of a large batch of 36 bought in 1900-1901 from Dick, Kerr and Co. They carried 22 inside and 34 outside. They were all fitted with top covers and open balconies from 1904 to 1916 and some were totally enclosed at a later date. Behind No. 1 is a single decker, and another open topped double decker is further down the street. The man on the bike with the fashionable 'skimmer' on his head seems to be riding on the wrong side of the road near the Gas Office corner. He may have been showing off to the group of women nearby, or perhaps he has been confused by the traffic lights (...only joking!). The wires spanning the street were attached to brackets fixed to the walls. To this day it is possible to see the stud holes. There were three systems of wiring in use from 1900. In North Bridge Street and Roker Avenue centre bracket poles were used until 1913 when they were replaced with side poles. In Fawcett Street there were span wires. In other areas there were side bracket poles.

SUNDERLAND. FAWCETT STREET   73153

Fawcett Street, 1944
This rather literary card is addressed to Miss Mather, 9 Southborough Close, Surbiton, Surrey.
"4 Upover
Seaburn Gardens
Sunderland
August Bank Holiday
This shows the principal street and Town Hall. Although the days have been dull and cool. The afternoons have been brightened by sunshine. The result is, in combination with the removal of some of the obstruction to the beach it is thronged with children having the appearance of vast numbers of flies as seen from the distance. It mischanced that I caught a cold and my friends coddled me with remedies with breakfast in bed for 3 mornings. I have not heard from Mrs. Sidney. Perhaps I may get some letter this morning. Love from Grandfather."

Of course the very best thing about Binns was the compressed air propelled bullet mechanism for delivering payment and bills and other items between departments and to the administration. This marvel was the Langson Paragon Transmitter. Langson Paragon was the name of the firm which supplied them. Another type could be seen at Blacketts. Their system employed wooden balls which unscrewed into two halves and into which were placed money and bills and so on. Then they were despatched along a complex system of rails. Such internal communication systems are still in use in some stores. For small children hauled along to Binns by their mothers at least the fascination of these mechanisms was a distraction from the apparently interminable 'Back to School' sales.

S.S. Eades's and C.J. Vincent
Vincent's Music Rooms and Piano Show Rooms. On the windows are advertised Rud. Ibach, Erards and Hopkinsons Pianos and Blutthner, Schiedmayer and Sohn, Karn Renowned Organs.

Fawcett Street

Fawcett Street

The Corporation only had a dozen single deck tramcars and it used them because they were the only cars which could get under the bridge at Tatham Street. The problem was that they had limited seating capacity. Quite early in their careers some of them were adapted to extend the seating capacity and to allow special provision for smokers. The problem with the smokers was that since the route was a short one they were prone to walking instead of taking the tram. "Serve them right. Do them good" you may say. However this preference for physical exercise cost the Corporation income! At a later date some of the single deckers were rebuilt as double deckers.

Fawcett Street looking south

Fawcett Street

There were several Maypole shops in Sunderland. They were grocers and delicatessens. On the awnings are advertised butter and tea. One of the most frequently recalled memories of the Maypoles was that they produced their own brand of butter and the counter assistants used to pat the butter into shape using wooden pats and a pattern was stamped onto the top of the butter 'pat'.

Fawcett Street and Bridge Street

This card is addressed to Mr. & Mrs. F. Cowling, 2 Courcy Road, Hornsey, London W8. "Dear F. & L. Sending your mat of (sic) tonight Monday 6 train from here. Sorry was not able to get it finished by Saturday last. So look out for it we are sending it by passenger train to London and let us know if you get it safe and how you like it. I know you will be having quite a busy time in your new home. From yours sincerely, Betty, with love."

Bridge Street

There goes another open topped double decker near to St. Mary's Church. The span wires across the street indicate that this is pre-1914 quite apart from other indicators. Trams could be quite dangerous. In the days of horse trams, derailments seem to have been quite common, and horses bolted occasionally with the tramcar still attached. The first incident when a person was run over by a tram was in Roker in November 1879 when a small girl was killed. Of course there were no one-way streets then or in the days of electric trams (except for Derwent Street). There was no such thing as a gyratory road system. Pedestrians crossed the roads at will, or just stood in the middle of them and chatted (or stared at the camera). Meanwhile the tramcar is a surprisingly smooth and quiet mover, and potentially quite lethal. The first accident involving electric trams was during the opening procession when No. 2 (operated by the vice-chairman of the Tramways Committee) ran into the back of No.1 (operated by the chairman)! Collisions were infrequent throughout the whole period of trams although as early as 1900 No. 10 (...driven by a depressed and suicidal driver) ran into the side of No. 3. Electric trams were better protected than horse trams regarding accidents involving pedestrians. They had lifeguard shields which could be lowered. However accidents will happen. The first involving an electric tram was in June 1903; a small boy as was often the case. Apart from people being run over others died when trying to steal rides on the step or hanging on to the back. Apparently Southwick boys were particularly good at this specialised form of surfing. It was also quite fashionable to injure yourself when trying to mount or dismount from a tram! Usually before it had stopped moving. Of course long and trailing dresses did not help matters. In fact if you have become addicted to the subject you would do well to read the book *Accidents and Incidents on Sunderland Tramways* written by Ed Keogh and edited by Arthur Staddon (North East Press). In fairness, and before we continue with our own tram journey, it must be pointed out that trams were remarkably safe vehicles and the number of accidents was very small in relation to the tram-miles covered and number of passengers carried.

Theatre de Luxe

The short-lived Theatre de Luxe was opened on the 29 April, 1912 but closed in 1917. It stood opposite the old Town Hall. It opened with the silent epic *Titanic*. No doubt the 500 (maximum) patrons were warmed up as usual with tea at the afternoon matinee. The audiences were entertained by the Bijou Orchestra between performances, or sinkings...! This card advertises prices of 7d for the best seats (children 5d) and 4d for the front seats. There were complete changes of programme, apparently, on both Mondays and Thursdays. Of course in those days there were continuous performances from 2.30 pm to 10.30 pm. People will remember the tendency to see films back to front! Arriving at the cinema half way through a performance then watching right through to the point of entry, then possibly leaving to catch an earlier tram home!

Theatre de Luxe reverse

Havelock Theatre

The Havelock Theatre, purpose-built as a cinema, was opened in 1915 on the site of the Havelock House which was destroyed by fire in 1898. Silent films were accompanied by a ten piece orchestra. It had the distinction of being the first cinema in Sunderland to be equipped for sound. *The Singing Fool* starring Al Jolson was the first talkie to be seen in Sunderland. It was shown between 15 July and 20 August, 1929. An amazing 120,000 people saw the film. It closed in 1963 after a brief period as the Gaumont. It was a very fine cinema holding 1,750 people in the circle and stalls and staffed for many years by an all male staff including pageboys in their blue uniforms and pill-box hats. The last film shown there was *The Three Hundred Spartans*. I remember it well ... Just along from the Havelock was the famous 'Messr. Meng Brothers, French Cooks, Confectioners etc.' Established in 1887, there was another branch at Ayr, Mengs was very well frequented:

"The spacious interior ... is admirably arranged and furnished in recherche style, small tables in the shop providing the requisite convenience for visitors partaking of light refreshments, such as tea, coffee, ices etc. At the back of this is a pretty tea room, very tastefully fitted, and beyond this is the handsomely appointed restaurant, where dinners, luncheons, etc. are daily served in first-class style from a well-selected and varied menu." Amongst their specialities Mengs included their 'bride cakes'. The Flemish-Gothic building was actually designed by Frank Caws, a keen experimenter with novelties such as terracotta and concrete. Its terracotta facade made it stand out very well.

Bridge Street

This is a beautifully clear picture. Opposite Mackie's Corner (where 'Sport Necessities' are for sale) is Newbegins. The strange masonic-style sign on the corner is actually that of Emersons the Opticians advertising 'EyeTesting' (you can just about make it out). The corner of Grimshaws Elephant Tea-House stands out very clearly. It was an eccentric design by the eccentric Frank Caws who actually envisaged the whole of Fawcett Street in such a Hindu Gothic style. It was one of the first buildings to use terracotta.

Bridge Street

This card is addressed to Mrs. Loveridge, Brockenhurst, Norbury Court, Norbury, near Croydon, Surrey. It is pleasing to see that the author had the right priorities!

"Dear J. Your postcard just received. Glad to see A.1. I had pleasant run up yesterday & have been to Sunderland today. Postponed Hartlepool till Friday."

Trams in Fawcett Street

No. 67 tramcar was a fully enclosed double decker which was originally purchased as a top covered tram with an open balcony in 1906. It and its five fellows were totally enclosed in 1922-23. No. 67 was withdrawn from service in 1953 which cannot have been long after this photograph was taken. Advertisements appeared on the outside of trams from March, 1921. In that year William Waples the advertising manager for Binns reached an agreement with the Corporation which resulted in the slogan 'Shop at Binns' being carried on the ends of the balcony trams. This was later extended to all of the trams, and the buses in later years. Waples was a very prominent freemason who is justly famous as a historian of freemasonry and because of his collection of photographs of freemasonry regalia. He also took many photographs of river and street scenes in Sunderland, and some of the most famous ones are attributable to him.

High Street

High Street East

This card is addressed to Miss E. Farnsworth, 20 Vane Terrace, Grange Iron Works, Durham, and is dated 1905. It has clearly been written in the rain because it is badly smudged, and this may well explain some of the slip-shod spelling.

"Dear Lizzie. Got your P.C. all right and we enjoyed ourselves well it was a bit windy & had a letter from Bee. Pleased to hear that you are enjoying your holidays it is raining very hard here … best regards and except the same from your friend"

The building in the foreground with the large wooden eagle emblem is still in existence and is occupied by Fairgreaves Mouldings. There was an inn on this spot as early as the 17th Century. In the 1850s it was the Royal Exchange and was managed by a Mr. Metcalfe who ran 'musical entertainments' in rooms towards the rear. Not entertaining enough, presumably, because Metcalfe's business failed in 1863, and a Mr. E.J. Newbigin took over. It was he who established both the Eagle Tavern and the Eagle Tobacco Factory. The former was described by Corder acidly as 'never an inn of interest or good class'. The property was taken over by Fairgreaves electrical engineering firm before the First World War. They were the first firm in the UK to manufacture bakelite, from 1913. The 6.5 foot high golden eagle (often mistaken for a griffin, or a phoenix) is now in exile on the island of Jersey following a long sojourn in a builders yard in Deptford. The Exchange Building stands further down the bank. The 'chaste, elegant structure' was designed by John Stokoe of Newcastle and built by George Cameron the grandfather of inventor Joseph Swan. Opened in 1814 it acted as a quasi-town hall and as a mercantile exchange. It was classical in style and built in stone with a stucco facade and a clock turret made of iron and timber. It was the scene of many important events in the history of the town. By the 1880s however it had fallen into decay, "a heavy dull stone building, for some years almost deserted". In 1889 it became the base of the Seamen's Mission whose efforts were described by the East End Commission as '... touching very closely the life of the district ...'

THE GENERAL POST OFFICE, SUNDERLAND.

The General Post Office

This is a Lilywhite Ltd. postcard. There is no message or date. One shop sign on the far side seems to read Attey. The two little girls in the right foreground with their arms linked are a nice detail. It may be post-1918 judging from the clothes. The Sunniside layout is actually quite old. It appears on Rains Eye Plan as Sunnyside. At least one of the buildings there today probably dates back to the 1780s. Women's dress lengths went down again briefly after the war in 1922-23 so they are not always an unambiguous guide. Future postcard interpreters will find present dress lengths no good at all. Women should think of these things.

Goodson's Ltd.

At 212 and 214 High Street. 'Mantles, Costumes, Largest Manufacturers in the United Kingdom. Branches in all Principal Towns'. This card is from the age of intensely corsetted, wasp-like narrow waists and of ostrich befeathered hats and head-dresses. No wonder she looks a bit grim.

Proclamation of King George V Procession in High Street East
Actually it is misspelt Proclamatioin. The police force followed by the boy scouts are going past Harrison and Co. (the Gentlemen's Boot Stores). Just beyond them is Hay and Tate. The card is addressed to Mrs. A. Dawson of 21 Sixth Street, Horden. The message reads: "Dear Alice just a line to let you know that we arrived at half past nine. And we enjoyed ourselves a treat and I hope you will let me know if you are coming on Friday. We are having terrible weather here with fog and rain. Kind love from all to your father and mother and all. From Alice." A confusion of Alices! It was a very popular women's name then of course.

Bridge Street
This card is addressed to a couple in Hull, Yorkshire. It may be dated August 1933.
"4 Thornhill Crescent, Sunderland. Dear Grace & Harold. Phew!! It is hot! I have not walked so much for ages. The air here agrees with me fine. Hope to be home tomorrow. Cheerio Petlet. Best love. Lil. XX."

Sunderland Lifeboat Parade

The event is dated 27 August, 1904. The curious message reads "They're laughing at yer, Geo. Hy. Fenwick. Jeanie wept." It is addressed to Miss Miller, c/o Mrs. Hooper, 9 Thornhill Gardens, Sunderland.

There seems to be a shop sign to the right which says 'Agency for Rudge Whitworth Cycles'. The right hand shop is a fishmonger. Next to it is Thomas Jopling with its signs 'Library' and 'Printer'. Further down is Fishers with the sign 'Umbrellas'. Between the fishmonger and Joplings the shop seems to be 'Pickerings'. It is not clear what the Fishmongers is called but their telephone number is 358 - because it says so to the right of the doorway! It may be a bit out of date now though.

Bridge Street

This has a message dated 1943 which reads "Having a grand time. Weather lovely. Both very sunburnt. Its very nice here & so near Hugh & see him at odd times. Will be home on Sunday. See you then. Love Mary." The address is not legible apart from Edinburgh. Just up from The Grand Hotel can be seen the trade sign of Haigs the Opticians.

Bridge St., Sunderland.

Bridge Street
Emersons the Opticians on the left are pushing their 'Eyesight Testing' (now try reading the bottom line please). The Queens Kinema stands out very clearly on this postcard. It opened on 2 December, 1913. It had a short life because competition from the Havelock brought about its closure in 1917. The manager for a time was the popular 'Uncle Joe' Andy a music hall artist whose proper name was George Andrew. Programmes, changed twice weekly, included such morsels as *Fatty Joins the Forces* and *Kum & Laugh & Scream* and *The Cry of the Captive*. There was tea in the balcony for patrons; free of charge naturally. George Andrew always wore full tails evening dress for performances. Female staff wore ankle-length skirts, blouses with large shoulder collars and bib aprons. The male commissionaires and pageboys were smothered in braid and brass buttons of course.

According to the shop window next door Christmas is on its remorseless way. As usual in these postcards most of the women are sweeping along briskly going about their business, while many of the men seem to have nothing better to do than stand around talking.

Bridge Street

"Travellers and tourists arriving at this busy Wearside centre will be well advised in making their headquarters during a brief or prolonged stay at the handsome and commodious establishment recently opened under the style of the 'Grand Hotel', and which offers perfectly up-to-date accommodation for either commercial or family visits to the town. Centrally situated within one minute's walk of the railway station, the 'Grand' has an imposing front elevation of five storeys." This advert in the 1902 *Coronation Souvenir* also drew attention carefully to the fact that 'The sanitary arrangements are completely in accordance with the latest scientific improvements ...'

Bridge Street, Sunderland.

Bridge Street

This view is over the old Stephenson bridge towards North Bridge Street. The name Black can be seen on the right. The Monkwearmouth Picture Hall, converted from the former St. Stephen's Presbyterian Chapel, was opened in May 1906 by George Black. It was later renamed the Bromarsh. It was the first permanent cinema of the town. The disused chapel was originally the home to Black's Waxworks Exhibition. Picture shows were put on there as early as 1904. The cinema was run by George Black Senior and his three sons who made up 'The Blacks Animated Picture Company'. Early pictures included items such as *An Irish Eviction, An Opium Eater's Dream* and *A British Cruiser in a Storm.* Occasionally films with foreign sub-titles were shown when there was a shortage of home produced movies and then a commentary was provided by a 'lecturer' such as Mr. Phil Roby. In 1916 it became the Bridge Cinema. In 1919 it was taken over by Will Marshall. Its new name Bromarsh was an anagram of Marshall Brothers (I suppose 'Marbroth' doesn't ooze with appeal either) It was destroyed by enemy bombs in 1943. The last film was *49th Parallel* starring Leslie Howard the very popular British actor who disappeared mysteriously on a flight between Spain and England. It has been suggested that his plane may have been shot down because it was believed by the Germans to be carrying Winston Churchill. Each in their own way the Blacks father and sons went on to enjoy very distinguished careers in the worlds of theatre and film production and television.

SECTION FOUR

AROUND THE TOWN CENTRE AREA

In this section we explore some of the main streets and areas connecting with Fawcett Street. En route readers we shall encounter a boy with a dining room chair, an unspeakable disaster, the architects Tillman, the Duke of Wellington, a fish perfumed railway station and a very practical use for a postcard.

Winter Gardens and Victoria Hall

This photograph is by Flintoff. It is an unusual view. The message reads "Dear Auntie. I am pleased to hear you are having such a nice holiday. We are nearly all tidy here now. Mammy went out for the first time yesterday. We all send our love to you and Uncle Jim. Eric. XX" It is addressed to Mrs. J.W. Gibbs, 6 St Mary's Avenue, Harrogate. The date is August, 1907. We will encounter the Central Library and Museum, the Winter Gardens and the ill-fated Victoria Hall elsewhere. The development of municipal parks and open spaces was prompted by the so-called Sanitary Question of the mid-19th Century. As early as 1854 Building Hill was purchased from the Mowbray family, whose fortune was derived from the coal trade. The first section of the park was laid out there and opened in 1857. An extension was added in 1866 on land bought from the North Eastern Railway.

YMCA Sunderland

On the front this card says "Thank you for last pc. I have not had one like it before". On the reverse the message is as follows:

"Glad you enjoyed Marsden Trip, we had a life boat procession & I could not have come to see you alone. I forgot to tell you how delighted mother was with those views Mrs. R. kindly sent her you must thank for mother. Hope you are all well now. Nellie." The card is addressed to Miss A. Redhead, 19, Equitable Street, Wallsend-on-Tyne and dated the 5 September, 1904. The lifeboat procession referred to here will be the one shown on page 51.

The building was designed by the famous Frank Caws (1845-1905) who was encountered earlier in this book when the 'Hindoo Gothic' Elephant Oriental Tea-House was considered. Caws was not only an imaginative architect he was also a generous man and much involved in charitable endeavours such as Lambton Street Boys Club and the YMCA. The YMCA had been established in Sunderland in 1871. It was originally accommodated in a house in Borough Road, then in Foyle Street. In 1878 a site on the corner of John Street and Borough Road was purchased. Much of the financial backing came from Edward Backhouse. The YMCA became so successful that the grand new building had to be extended twice in the next twenty years.

Borough Road

The Central Library and Museum in Borough Road was opened in 1879. There had been a Subscription Library in Sunderland from 1795 and this housed from 1810 a small Subscription Museum. In 1846 the Museum was taken over by the Corporation (which can claim to be the first Corporation to have implemented the 1845 Museums Act). It was housed in the Athenaeum Building to which it had been moved in 1840. In 1858 it was joined by the Public or Free Library. Initially it was for reference purposes only and there was no public access to the shelves. In 1879 the grand new Library and Museum was opened in Mowbray Park. The architects were J. and T. Tillman. The Library and the Museum were managed separately until 1906 when they were both brought together under Charlton Deas who introduced many welcome changes such as the abolition of access charges to the Museum, the introduction of a programme of temporary exhibitions and was responsible for the opening of a number of branch libraries. There was not open access to the shelves until 1911. Until then an indicator board had to be consulted by prospective borrowers. The first 'open access' library in the North East though was that opened at Hendon in 1908.

FREE LIBRARY, BOROUGH ROAD, SUNDERLAND

Free Library, Borough Road
One of the older single decker trams is passing the Central Library and Museum. In the background is the Palatine Hotel. Beside the Library is the taxi-cab hut with some horse drawn cabs standing beside it. A healthy horse on a reasonable diet deposits between four and six tons of manure per year. Multiply that by the large numbers of horses in the urban streets of Victorian and Edwardian England and you can see that pollution is not a new problem but has merely adopted a new form!

SUNDERLAND IN WINTER.

Sunderland in Winter
"17 Belle Vue Pk, Sunderland
Dear Miss Bastiman
I feel a great deal better for my holiday, and wish I was back. It is a horrible wet night and nothing to do. I remain your loving friend, Dorothy." The card is addressed to Mrs. Bastiman, 68 Louthfield Road, Middlesbrough. The date is not clear. The message is timeless! However one is unlikely to send a Christmas scene outside the months of late Autumn-Winter.

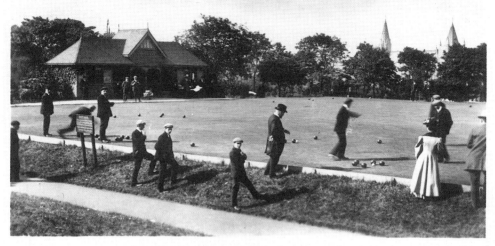

S 2688   BOWLING GREEN, MOWBRAY PARK, SUNDERLAND.

Bowling Green, Mowbray Park

The date seems to be 1909. The message reads:

"My Darling Wife. All well love, got nice order. Snowdon has got one too, both doing very well. All my love and kisses. Your own boy. Bertie." It is addressed to Mrs. Dutton of Eddington Road in Lytham, Lancashire. This is a real bowling action shot!

Winter Garden and Lake

At the rear of the Library and Museum was a large conservatory with tropical plants. It was destroyed in 1941 by the impact of the same bomb which damaged the Victoria Hall to such an extent that it had to be demolished. At the time of writing National Lottery funding had been achieved for the purpose of building a new Winter Garden.

Victoria Hall and Mowbray Park

It was at Victoria Hall on the 8 January, 1872 that the first 'moving picture' show was given, and it was also there that the Tussaud Exhibition provided the first glimpse of the new Animated Photographs on the 4 May, 1896. The show included, apparently, *An Operation in a Dentist's Chair, Blacksmiths at Work in a Forge, Ejection of a disorderly Person from a public house* and *An American lynching scene*. Fortunately for decorum the programme of the Victoria Hall also included a Ladies' Band. In fact this was not the first such show in the region because it had previously been seen in Newcastle. The Hall was bought by the Corporation in 1903 for £8,000 and modernised for a further £30,000. The New Victoria Hall then had two new halls where dinners and dances could be held and a suite of luxury reception rooms. It had electric lighting throughout, and a giant Vincent organ. It continued in its new found role of cinema as well. It was destroyed by an enemy landmine in April 1941.

Victoria Hall and Childrens Memorial, Sunderland.

Victoria Hall and Children's Memorial
The Victoria Hall was designed by G.G. Hoskins of Darlington and built in 1870-72. In 1906 it was very much enlarged by the local architect Eltringham. By then of course it had acquired an awful notoriety. On the 16 June, 1883 there was a show on at the Victoria Hall provided by the travelling entertainer Alexander Fay. Of the audience of 2,000 children about 1,100 were in the gallery. At the end of the show large numbers of children flooding down the winding staircase were confronted with an inward closing door which was soon jammed by the press of small bodies and 183 children were crushed and suffocated to death. The little gravestones of some of these children can be seen in Fulwell Cemetery. The very touching memorial was originally erected in Mowbray Park but was later moved to Bishopwearmouth Cemetery. At the time of writing there were plans to move it back again to the original site in Mowbray Park.

Wotan (One Watt) Lamps
Trade card of Davison Taylor, Plumber and Electrician, 4, Athenaeum Street & 10, Borough Road. The message reads "Dear Stan. Don't pay that cheque if you haven't. I've got a reduction. Can't leave shop. Kind regards. Davie." It is addressed to W.S. Atkinson, Blandford Street.

Sunderland Museum

Holmeside

This is a very clear image. Just visible is the shop sign of Laidler, Robsons and Co. who "... are pleased to undertake the Complete Decoration and Furnishing of Rooms, Houses etc. The Advantage of placing the Entire Scheme in the hands of one competent firm, cannot be overestimated, assuring as it does a perfectly harmonious tout ensemble, and materially minimising the cost. Estimates, Designs and Suggestions Gratis." On the corner is Maynards Ltd. Toffee Makers. Just in front of Maynards, rather incongruously, is a boy carrying a dining room chair! Perhaps it is a reject being returned to Laidlers! On the left is Turveys Garage. The enclosed double decker tram is one of a type whose end windows could slide round in a groove, a basic form of air conditioning. You can tell by the larger number of narrow window panels.

Stockton Road
"34 Ellerslie Terrace 28/12/1907. Wishing you many happy returns of the day. With kind regards from Mrs. Fortune and family. PS. Letter to follow for Mother." The card is addressed to Martin W. Harding, Village Farm, Salcombe, South Devon.

Waterloo Place
It seems to be addressed 22 June, 1917. The message is in French. The card is addressed to Mademoiselle Marguerite Jacob, Rue des Bassins, Dunkerque, France. The shop signs to the left read Marshalls Stores and Marshalls Photo Dealers. Then there is an Antiques sign. On the other side of Blandford Street is a sign which reads Lambton Landsale, L.D. Chatt and Sons. Beneath that is S. J. Scott for Smart Millinery. Beyond that is Chas. Grimshaw and Sons. On the right side is a sign for Mr. J. Boddy. One of the posters (just beneath the smoke) is for Swan Vestas. There was obviously no traffic problem then! Unless all the motorists are as bemused by the traffic system as today. The stamp was put on the front side of the card.

WATERLOO PLACE, SUNDERLAND.

Waterloo Place

"Dear Mary. Thanks for letter of this morning. I was so sorry that letter was delayed, & it was unkind of you to think that I was gone on leave elsewhere, had I not received letter yesterday. I would have sent these two cards to ask why you had not wrote & I hope Dear, you don't think I was to blame. Although I ought to have acknowledged the receipt of papers, before. I thought you were annoyed, by the letter today, as the stamp was standing to attention. Hope to hear again soon. With Love from Fred. XXXXXXXXX." There is no address so this will have been sent in an envelope probably. No date is given. The message has all the breathless incoherence of a worried lover explaining himself. It is to be hoped that she forgave poor Fred!

The town has several connections with and reminders of the Duke of Wellington who was not only the most famous soldier of his era but also a prominent politician. His brother Gerald was the Rector of Bishopwearmouth from 1827-48. There is also Douro Terrace which commemorates one of the titles of the Duke (the Marquis of Douro).

Vine Place

"Sunderland, Sunday, 4th March 1917

My dear Mother. May go out to France tomorrow or Tuesday. Thought we were going today. Have you heard from Geoffrey? I wrote to him yesterday. How's Father? Quite well I hope. Guess you'll like card. Hope you are fit and well - I am as. Best wishes & fondest love. Your devoted son, John. Keep Smiling J.S.G." The card is addressed to Mrs. Greenbank, 'The Orchard', West Field Road, Hemsworth, nr. Wakefield, Yorkshire. On the corner is a paper boy selling a newspaper. An advert for the Northern Laundry and Wear Dye Works of St. Marks Road can be seen.

Vine Place

A view down Vine Place. There is an advert for Bicycles and Motor Cycles on the gable end at the top right. It may be Rudge Whitworth. To the right is Todd and Son, Printers and Stationers. This is one of the vast number of Lilywhite postcards. The message reads: "Dear T.D.S. You will see by this view we are all well. Hoping you are the same. Yours affec. S.R.W." It is addressed to Mrs. S. Langton of 21 Park Road, Devonport, Devon. It is dated 13 May, 1921. It is not easy to see why a view of Vine Place should be a sign of good health!

SUNDERLAND. CENTRAL STATION. UNION STREET.

Central Station, Union Street

The detail of Corders Store is very clear. William Bell, the architect of the NER from 1877 to 1922, designed the Gothic clock tower and the brick facade of the station on the High Street side which were built in 1879. The former was a late addition to the design which arose from denunciation by the local press of a 'contemptible' scheme which would not match the status of the town. *Echo* campaigns on behalf of an 'outraged' public are not new! The old North end of the station is always recalled by Sunderland people as 'smelling of fish'. One of the great entertainments for children for many years was the weighing machine. There was also a gadget with which you could stamp out your name and other details on a metal tag. Simple pleasures!

Sunderland Station NER Illuminated and Photographed by the Kitson Light
"Am writing. Florence." It is to be hoped that Miss K. Loew of South Africa liked this card, and was satisfied by the extremely brief message!
"N.E. Ry Engineer's Office, Newcastle, January 13th, 1904. LIGHTING AT SUNDERLAND STATION: KITSON LAMP.
I have taken out particulars of the cost of the lighting at Sunderland

SUNDERLAND STATION NER ILLUMINATED & PHOTOGRAPHED BY THE KITSON LIGHT.

Station. There are 33 lamps, which burned altogether 17,460 hours. The oil and mantles cost £36 4s 0d, and the wages for maintenance etc. amounted to £8 10s 0d. Total £44 14s 0d. This works out at three farthings per lamp per hour, which is decidedly cheap. Yours truly, CHARLES A. HARRISON (Chief Engineer, N.E.R. Co.)." It is addressed to Capetown to Miss K. Loew, Van Reenen Esq, Joosteuksq, Muldersvlei. This has to be in the running for an award as 'Most Boring Postcard.' There were ticket offices at both ends of the Station and the tickets issued were distinguished by the letters N and S.

HIGH STREET WEST AND BEYOND

We have already glimpsed down High Street East. Now we wander up High Street West and, while we are there, continue into Hylton Road and Chester Road for good measure. In this section we encounter a love-sick Russian sailor, a brace of stone owls, a squaddie with magical powers and the architects Milburn.

Cobden Exchange Fire, 27 August, 1904

In fact this is J.A. Kennedy's Department store following the most dramatic event in its history. The public house on the left was the Rose and Crown, and Bass is being advertised on the windows. The message reads "I think this will be interesting to you Bob". It is addressed to Mr. Thomas Hudson, Scruton, Bedale. The building was named after the famous free-trader and Radical MP Richard Cobden. Before it was occupied by Kennedys it was used by a Thomas Beardall, a specialist in 'pretty bonnets'. In fact the building had been designed by the ubiquitous Frank Caws. Not only was Caws an advocate of terracotta he was also a fervent believer in concrete flooring. The Cobden Exchange had concrete floors, and Caws claimed that it was indestructible. In fact the basic structure did survive the fire and Kennedys was rebuilt and continued in use as a department store.

High Street, Mackie's Corner.   Sunderland.

Mackie's Corner
The name of Mackie's Corner derives from a silk hat manufacturer of the earlier 19th Century. Of course dangerous mercury was used in those days in the production of hats, and it is to be hoped that Mackie wasn't 'As mad as a hatter' as a result! Mackie's adverts can be found in the *Sunderland Herald*:

EXHIBITION OF MACKIE'S EXTENSIVE STOCK OF HATS, CAPS etc.
AT HIS NEW HATTING ESTABLISHMENT
Nos. 1 and 2 Hutchinsons Buildings
Early inspection is invited
A GREAT SAVING is gained by Parties buying their hats from the manufacturer

High Street West
This card is addressed to Miss F. Warden, 18 Grosvenor Place, Margate.
"Partridge Green, Sussex Jan. 3/1911. Dear Friend. Many thanks for your last. Please accept my best wishes for a very happy & prosperous New Year. Kind Regards. Yrs. Sincerely."

The tram is No. 31 and it is on the Circular route. This was one of the large batch of 36 trams bought from Dick, Kerr and Co. in 1900-1901. Open topped originally, they were all fitted with top covers and open balconies between 1904 and 1916. A few of them were totally enclosed later.

High Street West

High Street

The message is in Russian. It reads as follows:

"10 January, 1935

Dearest darling,

January 12th we are leaving Sunderland for Marseilles. So far I haven't got a single letter from you. I am very worried about your health. Many of the lads have got letters. I'm in good health. Everything is fine. Yesterday I sent you a sealed letter by airmail. Much love darling, as always Yours Vasilii.

Miss you, Fainochka, my dearest. A big hug. Vas'ya."

Vasilii and Vas'ya are the same person in fact! The latter is merely an affectionate form of the full name, just as we might call someone 'John' or 'Johnny'. The card is addressed to 'USSR, 25th of October Avenue, Block 38, Flat 76B, Faina Alexandrovna GRESHNER', that is to say in an order which is the reverse of English practise. There is no indication as to what the job of Vasilii was but it seems likely that he was a seaman. Hopefully a letter from Faina was in the post and on its way.

High Street
"Not the best street."
Well thank you! This is an odd message to send on a postcard even if it is true. Of course as the town grew and the Fawcett Street-Bridge Street axis became more significant the converse result was the progressive deterioration of High Street and Low Street. You can see the same thing happening today as Fawcett Street loses out to the Bridges shopping mall and to the traffic system.

High Street

High Street West
There is no date or message. It seems to have been tinted or coloured in places and that has lost some of the fine detail. It's a nice picture though. There is a very obedient sheep dog sitting at the road side to the right. It seems to be 1940s or 1950s.

High Street
The view is towards the west end of High Street West. The date is blurred but may be 1920 and the message is in Italian. Roughly translated it seems to say "All my love and thoughts my dearest." The address is in Ancona. It is written to a Signorina Maria Mengucci. There is a sign to the left which says Dean the Up-To-Date Tailor. Other signs indicate Strothers (far back and above to the right), Tylers, Wilson and Sons. The latter were 'Artists in Stained Glass' and 'Dealers in Fine Arts'. If you want any more you can read it yourself!

Right: Miss May Gibson, 'Silverstar'

Reverse of Beauty and the Beast
"Don't miss seeing THE BEAUTIFUL FAIRY PANTOMIME - BEAUTY and the BEAST. AVENUE THEATRE, SUNDERLAND. MONDAY, MARCH 26th." It is addressed to Miss Amy Shaw, Opera House, Harrogate. The Avenue Theatre, a 3,000 seat theatre in Gillbridge Avenue, was 'designed and built with special attention to its exits, and it is considered to be one of the safest buildings of its kind in the country'. The Avenue was opened as a theatre in 1882 by Richard Thornton the brother-in-law of the cinema pioneer 'Jimmy' Tindle. Sir Henry Irving made his farewell appearance here in 1904. Competition from Thornton's own Empire Theatre proved too much for the Avenue and it was closed down briefly. Moving pictures were shown there from 1908 when it was leased by Tindle. In 1916 audiences were excited and titillated by the *Perils of Pauline*. It closed down in 1932. The site is now occupied by Vaux Brewery.

Mr. and Mrs. H. B. LEVY and J. E. CARDWELL'S
"BEAUTY AND THE BEAST."

MISS MAY GIBSON, "SILVERSTAR."

73

Procession near the Londonderry

In fact this seems to be the Victory Peace Procession following the First World War from which a number of postcards were produced. The Londonderry had been the Peacock until 1831 and was an important coaching inn and a meeting place for Free Masons. There has been an inn on this site since at least 1772. In the 19th Century it was run first of all by a George Welford and then his wife from 1831, then it passed to John Patterson and from him to John Sidgwick in 1853. Sidgwick's price list sought to "... inform his numerous friends and the public generally that he has on hand a large and well selected stock of wines and spirits, guaranteed unadulterated." From Sidgwick's wife it passed to the Waddle family from 1887. They were the last publicans of the old Londonderry.

Procession near the Londonderry

This also seems to be the Victory and Peace Procession. The present Londonderry was built in 1901. The name dates back to 1831 and commemorates the opening of the harbour at Seaham. It replaced an older inn, the Peacock. It was built to a triangular pattern to fit into the junction of three roads. The first licensee of the new Londonderry was James Walker who held it only until 1906. Then it was taken over by Richard Duncan until 1954 who was one of the longest serving publicans of the town.

Empire Theatre, Sunderland.

Empire Theatre

"Dear Lilian. There is a panto on here & it is a real treat ... Johnny." The card is addressed to Miss Lilian Barlow, Holly Lodge, Shyness, Lincs. It is dated 31 January, 1917.

The Empire foundation stone was laid by Vesta Tilley on 29 September, 1906. It was officially declared open by her on the 1 July, 1907. It was established by the famous Richard, or 'Dicky', Thornton. The former Marsden busker from South Shields had made a great success of the run-down Union Street Music Hall in South Shields then went on to take over the Avenue Theatre and the Theatre Royal in Sunderland. Then in partnership with Edward Moss he went on to establish Empire Palaces throughout the north where the emphasis was on a flexible admissions pricing, accommodation and performances of good quality and respectable family entertainment. The Sunderland Empire Palace though was Thornton's own venture. It was built for him by the local architects W. and T.R. Milburn. The cupola was topped by a revolving steel globe surmounted by a statue of the Greek goddess of dance Terpsichore, holding a wreath. She was removed during the Second World War. The original statue is now inside at the head of the main staircase and a replica stands in her place. Of course in those days each of the categories of patron entered by different entrances to avoid any social embarrassment! The queues were entertained by buskers and were tempted to buy hot potatoes and hot chestnuts. In the interval, if you managed to get in, there was the opportunity not only to refresh yourself with beer and spirits but also with hot bovril. The most successful early years of the Empire were in the 1920s when a decline in attendances began.

Ralph Knox, Castle Street

Hudson
Ironmongers, Tools, Cutlery,
Garden Accessories.

Reverse of Business as Usual
Advertised as "Mr. Harry Day (by
arrangement with Moss Empires,
Ltd.) presents the London
Hippodrome phenomenal success
'BUSINESS AS USUAL'. A
COMPLETE TRIUMPH. EMPIRE
THEATRE, SUNDERLAND.
Monday, July 26th, 1915, and
during the week." The card is
addressed to J. Burnhope, 37
Johnson Street, Sunderland. It
bears the scrawled message
'Business as Usual'.

POST CARD.

JOHN WADDINGTON, LTD. GT. WILSON STREET, LEEDS.

MR. HARRY DAY
(by arrangement with MOSS' EMPIRES, Ltd.)
presents the London Hippodrome phenomenal success

"BUSINESS AS USUAL"

A COMPLETE TRIUMPH!

EMPIRE THEATRE, SUNDERLAND
Monday, July 26th, 1915, and during the week.

Business as Usual

Address on this side.

Halfpenny
Stamp.

*J. Burnhope
37 Johnson St
Sunderland*

Alf's Button 'Strike me Pink!'
The story of Alf's Button seems to have been an imaginative variation on the old theme of the Genie and the Lamp.

Reverse of Alf's Button
At the Empire Theatre. Commencing Monday, March 29th. A Martin Henry production. "If it's laughter you're after see 'Alf's Button' THE FUNNIEST PLAY OF THE CENTURY. ACTUAL LONDON COMPANY."

POST CARD.

Stamp.

EMPIRE Theatre,
SUNDERLAND.
Commencing Monday, Mar. 29th,

6-40—Twice Nightly—8-50.
6-0—Good Friday—8-10

A Martin Henry Production.

If it's Laughter
You're After—

See

"Alf's Button"
The Funniest Play of the Century

ACTUAL LONDON COMPANY.

Chester Road West, Sunderland.

Chester Road West

In 1894 the Sunderland Tramways company offered to construct a new line up Chester Road in return for a new 21 year lease. In fact the Corporation decided to take over the system itself and to begin electrification. The Chester Road extension of the New Durham Road route was the first to be installed by the new regime. A new depot was added in Hylton Road to supplement the one at the Wheatsheaf.

To the left can be seen the buildings of the General Hospital which were also designed by the ubiquitous Milburns. The Milburns were amongst the leading architects of Sunderland from the late 1880s to the early 1930s. In Bishopwearmouth they designed the Empire Theatre, the Fire Station and the Magistrates Court. Indeed the village centre of Bishopwearmouth has been described as 'Milburnopolis'. They were also responsible for the General Hospital, Bede School (now City College), the Water Company offices in John Street, the Little Sisters of the Poor Home, the Children's Hospital, Langham Tower, Burn Park Methodist Church and many housing estates including High Barnes. William may also have designed the porch of the Royal Infirmary with its wise owls gazing down on passers-by. Owls usually figured in the Milburn hospital designs. William claimed that it was because they were the 'patrons of constipation'!

The General Hospital belonged to the Poor Law Board of Guardians until 1929. The workhouse had been opened there in 1855 and the buildings became more and more elaborate as the hospital and educational provision was developed in accordance with a more liberal policy regarding the treatment of the destitute. The old buildings of the original workhouse were demolished in 1971.

Chester Road

Chester Road
"My dear Gerty. This is just a line to let you know I have received the beautiful flowers you sent me. They are just simply lovely, and I thank you very much indeed. I will write you a letter later in the week. Perhaps it will be Sunday when I write as we are Xmas cleaning and I am kept pretty busy all through the week. There I will wish you goodbye thanking you again for flowers. Love from Nora XXX. This is the road I am living in, but our house isn't on it it is higher up, ta ra. XXXXXXX."
The card is addressed to Peterborough.

*Your Meat Man ... Thos. Purvis,
Butcher, Sunderland*
The butchers were in Chester
Road.

YOUR MEAT MAN.

THOS. PURVIS, BUTCHER, SUNDERLAND. TEL. 1334.

Hylton Road

HYLTON ROAD, SUNDERLAND

81

'Our Kippers are Delicious'
Guthrie's Fish Shop.
Mrs. Guthrie poses outside her
shop in Silksworth Row.

Fish filleters
Mr. Guthrie in the back yard of
the shop. Jane Wilson (née
Lamp) is on the right holding
the fish's tail.

The Wounded soldiers. Victory and Peace Procession, 19 July 1919
There is no message. It is not very clear where this is. It may be the bottom of Hylton Road.

'Peace'. Victory and Peace Procession, 15 July 1919.
This seems to be in Hylton Road. The horses are harnessed in tandem which is a style which is only seen at horse shows and fairs nowadays but seems to have been quite normal in the 19th Century.

The Opening of Barnes Park, 1909
"Dear Dora. Many thanks for P.C. I am coming in a fortnights time for my holidays. Hope it doesn't snow when I do come. Yours Arthur."

The card is addressed to Miss D. Layfield, Bridge Farm, Catterick Bridge, Nr. Darlington and dated 20 September, 1909.

The land originally belonged to the Pemberton family who also, until recently, owned much of the land in the High Barnes area. They were a quite extensive clan whose wealth derived originally from coal exporting and from mine ownership. They were principal partners in the Wearmouth Colliery. Pembertons owned other substantial properties in the region including the mansion which ultimately became the Ramside Hall Hotel and another one in the attractive Hawthorn Dene which was demolished in the early 20th Century. The house in Barnes Park stood where the bowling greens are today. For some time it was used as a girls school. It was demolished in 1921. Very recently the ceremonial gold key used to open the park was bought by a Whitburn lady at a Christie's auction. There was a long twenty year campaign to have a park established there. In 1904 the land was bought from a Mr. Punshon by Colonel Thomas Reed a member of the Sunderland family which had a very successful printing and publishing firm and the chairman of the parks committee. He paid £8,500 for the land. The park was laid out by 2,798 unemployed men supervised by skilled gardeners. It was opened on the 6 August, 1909 and the key was presented to Colonel Reed.

THE WHEATSHEAF AND ROKER

Back across the Wearmouth Bridge now, and on to Roker. Much of the land of Roker, Seaburn, Fulwell and Monkwearmouth was originally part of the estate of the Williamson family of Whitburn Hall whose link with the town dates back to the time of the English Civil War, and the fortunate marriage of a royalist gentleman and the daughter of a parliamentary officer (commemorated most obviously in the name Dame Dorothy Street). Here we will encounter the once substantial tourist trade of Roker and Seaburn as our postcards take us into a land of sun, sand and stout. Naturally there are very many postcards of the Roker and Seaburn area because tourists and holiday makers are a major market. You could easily gain the impression that the population of Sunderland spent most of their time on the beach in warm sunshine. It was only from the late 19th Century that Roker began to develop as a residential area. Until the 1880s it could only be approached through the working class suburb of Monkwearmouth, and that area was avoided by the middle class.

Roker Park
The message is addressed to Mrs. D. Parr of the Issue Section, Regional Petroleum Office, Church Street, Nottingham. It is dated 10 July, 1945.
"Aren't you jealous of the nice weather and me enjoying it while you're all in the office all the time? Is Mr. Lambton back? I hope he is OK now. See you Monday. E.D."

Wheat Sheaf
This card is addressed to Mrs. Peacock, 30 Victoria Street, Goole, Yks. It is dated 8 February, 1907.
"Dear Aunt. Has your letter stuck on the way this week. How are you getting on. We are fine. Ethel."
Two early open topped double decker trams can be seen. They are probably en route to Roker or Fulwell via Roker Avenue. The imposing tram offices are on the right with the tram sheds to the right of them and partly masked by a tram.

Tram
This card is addressed to Mr. S. Burrell, 17 Nicholson Street, Sunderland. It is dated 2 March, 1910.
"Dear Sam. I received your letter, sorry I could not send you the postcard on as I have no more finished. I don't get any done when I'm on day duty but I will bring some through Saturday. Let me know when I have to come. Yours F. Edmundson.

Roker Avenue

The message is dated 25 July, 1911 and addressed to a Miss M. Herring, Albion house, Cross in Hand, Sussex.

"Dear Paul. How goes it with you? As ages have elapsed since I last had any news from you. Am having a great time up here and had a splendid voyage. Hope it will be as nice coming back. Give my love to Jack and Stanley and all the others. Am thinking of going to the sea this afternoon. It only costs a 1s. In fact we are quite close to it. Goodbye. Write soon. With best love. Winnie."

The Wheatsheaf Hotel seen here was built around 1904 on the site of an earlier coaching inn. The lighthouse was a famous landmark, a wooden 'folly' which was a replica of the famous octagonal lighthouse which stood on the North Pier until 1902. That was demolished when it began to lean alarmingly as a result of splits in the roundhead of the old north pier caused by a deepening of the channel. There was a light in this wooden replica but it was not allowed to be used because it could be misinterpreted from the sea as a genuine navigation light and vessels might (presumably) have strayed up Roker Avenue. The wooden lighthouse was the emblem of Wills Lighthouse Stores which was originally to be found within. The firm was a Wholesale and Retail Grocers and Provision Merchants: Importers and Manufacturers. Later on the building was occupied by Walter Willsons. Its last occupant in the 1950s was Marley's Sweetshop with its myriads of tantalising glass jars of sweets.

WHEAT SHEAF CORNER, SUNDERLAND.

Wheat Sheaf Corner

This is one of many Lilywhite Ltd. Postcards. It is a good view of the area at what appears to be 4.20 pm. The date is not clear. It may be 1921. It says Wills on the roof of the Lighthouse Building. The message reads:

"To F.M.M. Just a card hoping I will find you all well as it leaves us. Received your letter this morning many thanks for the same. I am suffering from the same complaint as you. That is the reason I am sending a card and I thought you would like another view of this place. Will write a letter in a day or so. Ta, Ta. Love to all. From Ethel." It is addressed to Miss M. Porter, Medina View, Stephensons Road, Cowes, Isle of Wight.

The Mill from Fulwell

The Mill from Fulwell

This is a popular angle for pictures of Fulwell Mill. The house to the right was demolished in the 1950s. It used to be occupied by a family called Moodie.

Newcastle Road, Sunderland.

Newcastle Road

This view is of Newcastle Road before the First World War and before it was developed.
The Fulwell Mill is a prominent landmark. It was built in 1921. It is the most complete mill
standing between Humberside and the Firth of Forth. It was last used in 1949, although an
engine was employed then rather than the wind vanes. The sails were replaced in 1986 and
the mill was reopened to the public in 1991. It is made of the magnesian limestone which is
predominant in this area. The church on the right is the Nationalist Spiritualist Church
today. However it was originally occupied by the Congregationalists and then by the
Welsh Presbyterians. The building was designed by John Eltringham and built in 1877. It is
Geometrical Gothic in character and was constructed in limestone with sandstone quoins
and dressings. Incidentally the best short introduction to places of worship in Sunderland
is the little booklet *Buildings and Beliefs* (Wearside Historic Churches Group, 1984) by
Geoffrey Milburn. *Below:* Reverse of card.

Monkwearmouth Parish Church

This card is addressed to Mrs. A. Rushforth, 81 Hanover Street, Dewsbury, Yorkshire. The date is possibly 1914 or 1919.

"Roker Sunderland. Dear Friend. Just a few lines you know I am having Holidays here & are having a good time. I hope you will enjoy yourself at Morecambe next week. This place is just a little nicer than Bridlington but 50 times nicer than Morecambe. Annie." It looks like Bridlington, anyhow it is eleven letters across starting with 'Brid'!

The North Aisle to the left of the tower was built in 1875. The glass canopy over the porch entrance was designed to preserve the Saxon porch but was removed as it was the cause of condensation which was causing more damage.

St. Peter's Church

"With love to my dear Father & Mother."

UPPER PROMENADE, ROKER.

Upper promenade, Roker

Horse drawn trams were used in Roker from 1879. The Corporation extended the electric tramways system to include Villette Road, Grangetown, Fulwell and Roker and Seaburn between 1900 and 1905. In 1937 a line was added from Fulwell via Dykelands Road to Seaburn as well. Here can be seen two open topped double decker trams. This dates the photograph to pre-1914. The nearest tram may be No. 64 which was supplied by Dick, Kerr and Co. in 1902. It and the other nine in that batch were all fully enclosed in the 1920s and 1930s. No. 64 continued in service until 1954. In 1900 trams were running every five minutes normally but every two and a half minutes in the busy holiday season. In fact the tram system was the key to the development of the resort.

Roker Pier

THE TERRACE. ROKER. SUNDERLAND.

The Terrace, Roker
One of the little girls is carrying an enamel bait can. The white painted bases of the lamp posts were part of the black-out precautions of the First World War. The smoking chimney at the extreme right will have been the Whitburn Paper Mill which was closed in 1933. The enclosed double decker tram is one of those with the curious window arrangement which allowed the end windows to slide along. Roker Terrace was designed by John Dobson for the Abbs family of Roker and was built in the 1840s.

THE TERRACE. ROKER. SUNDERLAND.

The Terrace, Roker
There is no message and no date. He seems an insolent looking urchin to the right though!

The Terrace, Roker

This card is addressed to Mrs. Tiplady, 6 St. Davids Road, St. Annes on Sea and dated August 1913. "Fire Station, Sunderland. Dear M. We are here once more having a splendid holiday. The weather is glorious. We spent one day at a farm, and we have to go to two flower shows, a nice change from the sea ..."

The row of bathing huts on the beach between the piers gave rise to the name of the Bathing Beach. There was also a floating diving board. The developers of the Roker Baths Hotel had visions of this area as the nucleus of a Spa Resort. The hotel was so-called because the owner pumped sea water into the building to provide hot and cold showers and steam vapour baths. It was believed that salt water was good for the constitution.

The Sands, Roker

This card is addressed to Master J.C. Cooper, The School House, Uppingham.

"This is rather a glorified view of where I took several Saturday walks last term. It is about two miles from Sunderland. I came up here on Wednesday."

This will be about 1904 because that was the time of the maze. Bathing machines can be seen on the bathing beach.

Sands and Pier, Roker
"Please forgive me for not writing to you about the costume. Box came to Cleadon yesterday. Going on to Newcastle on Sat. Hope you are having a good time at work. Lovely weather so far. Edith." The card is addressed to Miss J. Watson, 28 Oxford Street, Holgate Road, York. The date is not clear.

There are fishermen's huts at the foot of Roker Bank with the upturned boat in front of one of them. The shadows suggest evening time as the sun is to the west. It makes you wonder why the beach is so busy at that time? It may have been a bank holiday. It looks pre -1914.

Lower Promenade, Roker
The sun is to the west again. The angled bank side to the left of the picture is the spoil that was removed from Brunel's Wearmouth Dock. The natural coast line is low limestone cliffs but between the Holey Rock and the Blockyard area the spoil from the dock changes the appearance of the cliffs in this way.

Pack your Bag and come to Sunderland

Pack your Bag
and come to   SUNDERLAND

Lovely scenes and vistas rare
Spread around me everywhere,
Some of the prettiest appear
Within the bag I send you here.

1239

Top of Promenade, Roker
This looks like *circa* 1910. Note the newspaper boy on the right. At this time Smith's donkeys were stabled behind the Roker Hotel. Later they were in stables adjacent to St. Benet's Church. When the donkeys' working day was done small boys flocked around to volunteer to take them back to their stables. Of course this was just a ploy to get a free ride because left to themselves the plodding little donkeys were so practiced in their routine that they were quite capable of returning to their stables. They could probably have collected the money too given the chance.

Full up Everywhere at ROKER

Full up Everywhere at ROKER
"Westbourne Road, S'land. Dear G.A. I am very pleased to hear you had one fine day. I really thought all the good weather was gone. I hope you are not in the same position as some of them appear to be. The weather here is very clear & can be very windy at times. I am sure all at home would be pleased when you managed to beat Tingley simply. Cricket is about over & we are looking forward to football. S'land have a very strong team this year and they will take some whacking ..." This is addressed to Mr. G. A. Whinfield, Grassmere House, High Street, Cleethorpes. The date could be August 1908.

Woman and child and donkey

THE BATHING PLACE, ROKER.

The Bathing Place

There is no message and no date. This area was known as the bathing place or the bathing beach. It will have been a hive of activity in July 1914 during CREMONA DAY:

MY DEAR BOYS AND GIRLS

Tomorrow is CREMONA DAY at Roker AND SEA LANE and no doubt you are all ready and have all made arrangements. All that we want is a FINE DAY, and, as you will no doubt remember, I want you to meet the CREMONA MAN either at ROKER TRAM STATION or SEA LANE TERMINUS at 3 o'clock and receive your CREMONA FLAG, then start building your castle.

Below I give you the rules GOVERNING THE COMPETITION. NOW ALL DO YOUR BEST to Build a FINE CASTLE, one fit for THE KING TO LIVE IN. You can add a FORT OR A MOAT or anything you like. There will be lots of STRANGERS there and just show them what SUNDERLAND BOYS AND GIRLS CAN DO.

By the way, it might be as well to remind you not to forget your CREMONA TOFFEE.

Yours sincerely
CREMONA

Pier and Lighthouse, Roker
The red and white striped lighthouse was ceremonially opened on 23 September, 1903 with the Earl of Durham in attendance. A polished black commemorative block was placed on the new lighthouse. In fact there is a lovely photograph of the event when River Wear Commissioners and RWC officers and staff together with VIP guests and partners are crowded around the lighthouse.

The Sands, Roker
"Sunderland. August 22nd. 2nd. Engineer SS *Bilton*. Dear Sir, we arrived safely here from Goteburg last Sat. but I have not had much time to write for enjoying myself, we sail again tomorrow for Laivig Norway, about 50 miles from Horten I guess. Accept my kindest Regards & Remember me to the Boys. Yours Sincerely. A. Grey." The card is addressed to a Kaptien Mariner in Horten, Norway. A postscript reads "This is our beach."

Sands and Pier, Roker

The great North Breakwater was a long time in coming. River Wear Commission engineers had been proposing such a development since as long ago as the 18th Century. In 1876 a thorough report on the subject proposed two breakwaters. Work began on the North Breakwater in 1885. Advantage was taken of a natural rock outcrop as a foundation but further out a foundation of rubble and cement had to be built up. The huge blocks were put in place using a 290 ton hydraulic crane. Along the whole length was a tunnel to carry the cables and act as maintenance access in bad conditions. The final blocks were put into place in 1902. One of them was actually laid by Ferdinand de Lesseps, builder of the Suez Canal, who visited Roker in 1889. The 2,800 feet long breakwater was finally opened in September 1903. Work started on the South Breakwater in 1893. With trade and RWC income in decline before the First World War it was decided to cut back on the original plan for twin breakwaters and to conclude work on the South Breakwater in 1912. It is not, despite popular belief to the contrary, unfinished.

Motor Boats and Sands, Roker

Holey Rock and Sands, Roker

"28/9/38. From Up-Over Seaburn Gardens, Sunderland. My dear friend. Hope interceded to drive me out yesterday but a general sea mist blocked out the landscapes. By way of change went to the pictures. The parks & promenade are brilliantly illuminated at night - but how long? If peace is broken they will I suppose be discontinued. The town's folk were crowding down to see them last night. I read of the underground stations being closed in places. I hope it will not disturb you. I've just heard from Clare. Aunt Lizzie seems to have travelled about. Hope I'll go there before Winter. Today we go to Stockton. Love to all from your loving Grandfather R.L. Lister." The card is addressed to Miss G.E. Mather, Garth, 9 Southborough Close, Surbiton, Surrey. A superscript reads "The rock here shown was blasted away last year."

The reference to the Illuminations is to the lights in Roker Park only because in 1936-38 they were only in the Park. There were illuminations again between 1949-54 and then 1986-93. When they were switched on in 1949 from the top of the Seaburn Hotel they immediately fused! The Verandah Cafe is still there today, but in the guise of a small pub. There was a verandah all the way around the cafe. There are seats in the bottom right for a concert party. Swings for the children (... and children at heart) can just be seen behind the shelters on the left. The buildings on the top of Cliff Park are approximately where the local Abbs farming family had their summer residence. It was also the site of the so-called Abbs Battery of the 18th Century. In the Second World War there was a small military camp there as well. Beneath grass beside the Bede Cross there are still the quadrants of two huge naval guns. Just below the Coast Guard look-out station can be seen a gun emplacement let in to the cliff face *a la Guns of Navarone*.

'Paddling'- at - Roker

"Dear Edwin. I am going to do this when you are looking at it. Love to Mother & Father. Tell mother to write. Annie. XXXXXXX." This is addressed to Master E. Lewis, 65 Cromwell Street, Newcastle-on-Tyne. The date may be July, 1913.

The proper word is, of course, 'plodging'. These are clearly plodgers. In the background are the caves of Holey Rock in the limestone strata. These caves were eventually collapsed in 1937 and the headland shortened to prevent more serious erosion undermining the cliff.

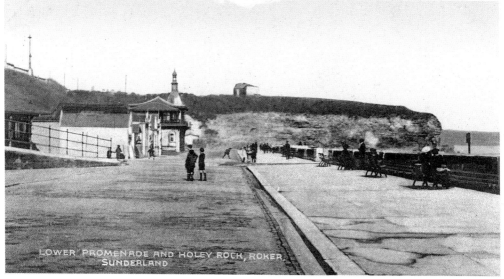

Lower Promenade and Holey Rock, Roker

It is addressed to Sister Gertrude Ann. The address is squeezed in to the very top of the card above the stamp frame and is 40 Church Street North, Monkwearmouth. There is no stamp on though. It reads "Just a few lines to tell you that I received your letter and thank you we are having glorious weather here plenty of sunshine. Yours Mary."

The 'Jumbles', Holey Rock, Roker

One of the groups of itinerant seaside entertainers who visited the various resorts in the Summer season. Anyone with any common sense, judging from this photograph, didn't pay the entrance charge but stood and peered over the fence. During performances a collecting box was reached out into the crowd on the end of a stick. One old lady who could remember them said "of course we just ran away"! You wonder how the Jumbles made a living. The Jumbles were more of a 'concert party' than the Pierrots *(opposite page)*. They entertained with a repertoire of songs, dances and sketches. This picture may be later than that of the Pierrots simply because of the better seating provision and the sliding canvas tilt over the seating.

Holey Rock

"Enjoying my holidays. XXXX. Just a note. Saw J. Lowe here on Saturday but he only stayed one day. Salmon season only fair as far as it has gone all well up this way. Weather very unsettled. From Cousin Jim." This card is addressed to Miss Sarah Lowe in Aberdeen.

The Pierrots, Roker

"Hope you were able to entertain the company on Friday Jessie, with your recitations. We are having lovely weather up here. J.D. Cott." This is addressed to Miss Jessie Mitchell, Nelson Street, Tayport. It seems to be date stamped 1906.

The Pierrots performed at Roker during the summer seasons in the period before 1914. They were self employed entertainers who let the public see snatches of their show as 'trailers' for the full event. The problem was that eventually most people had seen most of their act in this way at different times. Not much is known about them. Certainly one of them was a Theobald Vickery, one of a Somerset family which emigrated to Sunderland around 1880 where they had relatives and lived in Gladstone Street. It may be that other members of the family took part in the Pierrots. A recently deceased member of the Monkwearmouth Local History Group, Jim Melton aged 96, could well remember watching them.

Holey Rock, Roker

"Dear Annie. Cards received this morning. Pleased you are having a nice time. Hope the weather continues to be fine. I expect to see you all rosy when you get back. Everyone is all right here only too much work. I will get a bit ease now as A. Pearce starts tomorrow. Nip in & enjoy yourselves. Hoping all are keeping fit. Best love Geo & Nan XXXX." This card is addressed to Mrs. Cadman, c/o Mrs. H. Roberts, 59 Mayfield Grove, Harrogate. Stamped 19 August, 1930. There was no punctuation originally! You should try reading it in one breath!

Of course the holes of Holey Rock, from which it derived its name, held a great fascination for children who would try and race backwards and forwards through them and beat the waves of the incoming tide. I suppose the nearest equivalent might be running across the road in front of traffic!

Holey Rock, Roker

"SS *Roman Prince*. Palmer's Shipbuilding Yard. Hebburn-upon-Tyne. Dear Miss Hume. I hope you are having a very pleasant holiday. I have been here quite a while now. We had a nice time in Dunkirk & London and had a week home from here. We came back on the 20th. And were at Muriels & were at the Glasgow Show with Sam and Effie Thursday. Still indefinite as to weather now unsettled and colder than we had. Hope you are feeling the better for your rest. Kindest regards from us both. Mrs. S. Nicol."

This card is addressed to a Miss Hume in Falkirk, Scotland. The date appears to be 1925. Probably as a result of a popular misinterpretation of the origin of the name there was a tendency to keep pieces of the rock as charms against the power of witches. Also, for those who believe in such things, it is advisable to collect a couple of those curious stones on the beach with holes bored through them by a rather strange sea creature and to tie a ribbon through the hole. If you do that you are guaranteed protection against most of the usual types of magic spells and tooth-ache or so I am told.

S.2678   THE CAVE. HOLEY ROCK. SUNDERLAND

The Cave, Holey Rock

The caves were potentially dangerous because the rising tide would fill the caves up to the height of the dark band on the stone. Children played in the dank and dripping caves at low tide. They were also the home to gambling schools of local card sharps. The flat sands outside were a good vantage point for uninterrupted observation for possible police raids. In a trice the gamblers could become innocent trippers and plodgers ... Just like these two in fact.

The Bridges, Roker Park

The Roker Ravine contains some fine caves and is itself a collapsed cavern. Mildly acidic water percolating through limestone dissolves and gradually widens cracks and fissures until potholes and caves are produced. In this case the sea has finished the job. Further incursion was stopped by the building of the Roker Low Promenade. The road bridge was built as late as 1880 and it was only then that there could begin the development of the sea-front in the form of fine terraced housing on Williamson land along the sea front. The wooden bridge is an example of the timber engineering and bridge construction of a local firm Messrs. Armstrong, Addison. It is actually in the *Guinness Book of Records* as the oldest creosoted bridge. It was made of telegraph poles from Riga and creosoted in North Shields. It was saved from demolition in 1983 by public subscription. The arched stone bridge was not opened until Roker Park was opened to the public. Before the stone road bridge was built the route to Whitburn was via Cleadon.

The Lake, Roker Park

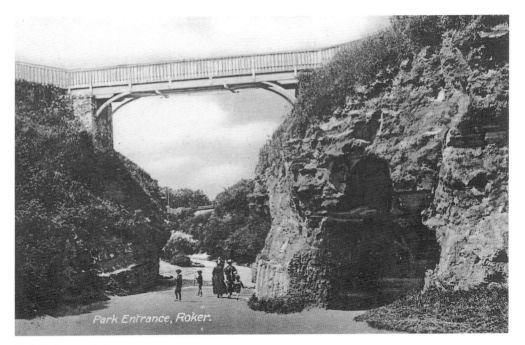

Park Entrance, Roker

Park Entrance, Roker
The cliffs are honeycombed with caves and crevices at this point. Indeed there are tales of tunnels as far inland as Hylton Castle! One of the caves was the famous Spottee's Cave. Spottee was, reputedly, a shipwrecked Frenchman who lived in the cave in the 18th or early 19th Century. In Hartlepool he would surely have been hanged! In Sunderland he became a legendary character who, no doubt, was sought out by curious children who embroidered the legend. The name 'Spottee' was derived, it is said, from his large spotted kerchief or from spotted clothing rather than problems of skin complexion. It is claimed that he gained a living as a wrecker; lighting fires on the beach and luring vessels to their doom! A busy man. The probability is that he was just a poor, muttering, tormented tramp. An account is given in James Patterson's *A Guide to Sunderland and Environs.* Spottee's Cave or the Monk's Hole is the largest and most imposing cave, the depths of which have never been completely plumbed. After attempts at exploration in the 18th and 19th Centuries the back was sealed off by the Corporation. It was used for storage purposes then as a set piece in the Illuminations. In recent years it has been marred by the construction of a pumping station.

The Bandstand, Roker

"Thursday night. My Darling. Just a few lines to thank you for the letter yesterday and the card today. I have started a letter, my love, which you will get as usual. I am keeping better, my pet, and am nearly my old happy self again. I hope you are a lot better my treasure, and very happy. Take care of yourself. Ever your faithful boy. Eric."

Roker Park was laid out after a gift of the land was made to the Corporation in 1880 by Sir Hedworth Williamson and the Church Commissioners.

The Bandstand, Roker

The present bandstand replaced the original uncovered one in 1904. It is a replica of a bandstand on the Thames Embankment. The general architectural style of bandstands tends to reflect an interest in Chinese garden architecture which took off in the mid-18th Century.

Roker Park, Sunderland, in Winter.

Roker Park in Winter

ROKER CLIFF PARK & PROMENADE

Roker Cliff Park and Promenade

This is certainly before the First World War. There is a covered tram which is open at the end. The Abbs Farm buildings are standing where the Coastguard Look-Out was later built. The tram is a fairly standard double decker. *Corporation Tramways Rules and Regulations* were published in July, 1900. Ticket Inspectors were required to 'regulate their watches daily with the Town Hall clock, which will be taken as a standard'. Conductors were advised to practice driving (unpaid and in their own time) until they were proficient enough to receive a certificate. They were required to call out the destination of the car and the principal stations. Signals were passed to the driver by means of a bell and a whistle. Conductors were told not to stamp on the floor as a means of signalling. They were also responsible for changing the reversible seat backs and the reversible destination boards at each terminus. The drivers were told to 'speak pleasantly to drivers of other vehicles when requesting them to move out of the way'. Note the side brackets used to carry the wires.

SEABURN

... and so to Seaburn, and journey's end.

Nowadays, even during the occasional burst of really hot and sunny weather, the sands of Roker and Seaburn are nothing like as busy as they were into the 1950s and it is not easy to understand the part they played in the social life of the town. For those of us who remember those days it seems like a Golden Age dominated by square green canvas tents, banana and sand sandwiches, the taste of very salty sea water and the queues at Seaburn Camp waiting for the bus or at the tram shelter across the road from Alex Hasting's at the end of another hard day on the beach.

Seaburn
The card is addressed to Mrs. A.M. Brown, 43 Cleveland Square, Hawtonville, Newark, Nottinghamshire. It is dated July, 1963. The message reads "Arrived Safe. Everyone here is OK. The weather is smashing. Eric, Ethel". This is a nice, almost idyllic view over the Funfair and the verdant lawns beyond to the sea.

Rough Sea, Seaburn
In fact this is moderate compared to what the sea can achieve when it really tries! It is not unusual to have stretches of promenade and tarmac covering ripped out by immensely powerful waves.

Extension Park, Roker
There is no date and no message. This is a good view back along the sea front. Of course thankfully the old tram terminus is still standing. At one time there was a very fine circular tram shelter opposite the end of Featherstone Street but that went the journey before we arrived at times which are more sympathetic towards such old buildings and structures.

New Promenade, Sea Lane
Note the ice cream man with his hand-barrow in the centre of the picture.

Seaburn Promenade
The date is probably the mid-1930s. The Seaburn Hotel used to have an illuminated sphere on its roof with an advert. This is not shown on this picture. A member of the Monkwearmouth History Group recalls that his uncle broke an ankle when he fell from the roof as he was helping with the installing of the sphere. Happy days! In the distance is the Bay Hotel.

New Promenade, Seaburn
"Dear All. I hope you are all well. I am playing truant this week. The weather hasn't been so bad so far, will be seeing you soon. Love to all, Isabel." The card is addressed to Mr. and Mrs. Scraffen, Hadston Row, South Broomhill, Morpeth, Northumberland.
A view of the site of the later Seaburn Hotel with an unmade road along to Whitburn. Cleadon Water Tower can be seen on the horizon.

Wading
"21/1/09. Dear Mary. Another for your collection. Hope you'll like it. Is fine weather here at present, hope it is the same yonder. Remember me to all at home. We had plenty of snow here last wk. but glad to say none about at present. Best respects to all. Your affectionate brother, Ted." The card is addressed to Miss M. Honey, Ellerslie, St. Sampsons, Guernsey.

CLIFF STEPS, ROKER.

Cliff Steps

"10 Cliffe Park. March 24th. I am so sorry to hear that you have got so bad with boils & sore throat. I do hope you will be better by the time you go on holiday. It would do you a good change. We are going for a long walk to Cox Green & back home by track for dinner. It is very dry and fine, not too windy. With best love and a Happy Easter from Micky M. Taylor." This is addressed to Miss Yeoman, 58 Upper Grosvenor Road, Tunbridge Wells. The handwriting is not very legible and the message is crammed into the small space. The date may be 1913. A walk to Cox Green and back for dinner from Roker is a canny walk by anyone's standards!

The famous cannonball rocks are quite visible. The level taken for building the promenade can be seen as well as the original cliff face steps.

SUNDERLAND. ROKER SANDS.

The Sands

The donkeys have been lined up to have their photograph taken. There is no date or message. It looks likely to be an inter-war card.

The Cliffs

The card is addressed to Crook, Co. Durham. It is written lightly in pencil and is not very legible. However the gist is as follows: "Dear Mother. Having a good time here. Had fine weather until yesterday and it never stopped raining all day. Write and let us know if you are coming on Monday".

Holey Rock

On The Sands
Three donkeys and two children. It makes you wonder what the collective noun should be for a group of seaside donkeys: 'A doze of donkeys' perhaps?

At Seaburn
"I went to Seaburn last week, went into the water, just to see if I could still float and I can! Fat ones and thin in the water. I thought I was going to get locked up for laughing at them. If Fred had been anywhere about I am sure I should have been put in clink." The authors name is not clear. The card is addressed to a Miss Blanche.

The Rocks, new Sea Wall

The spherical rock formation is reminiscent of cannonballs and that is what provides the name for the area. The rock formation was thought to be unique to the Roker and Seaburn area. However there are also outcrops in Madagascar and in Australia. So it is unique-ish. The concretionary limestone was chemically precipitated 260 million years ago in the Zechstein Sea. Although there are no fossils the incompatible action of two carbonates, calcium and magnesium, coming out of solution together on the sea bed, has caused weird and wonderful shapes. The spheroid 'cannonballs' are packed tightly in a soft dolomite matrix which powders easily. The result of the combination is also the strange honeycombed rocks seen in countless local rock gardens and drystone walls. The tiny cavities have been produced when one of the carbonates has dissolved.

Sea Lane

The name 'Seaburn' is fairly recent. In the 1930s the area was known simply as Sea Lane after the road which ran from the front to Sea Road. It appears that the original Sea Lane ran all the way from the Blue Bell down Chichester Road and the 'Corkscrew Bank' to the present Seaburn Hotel. Certainly that route is referred to as Sea Lane on old 19th Century Ordnance Survey maps. Indeed according to some views the term included the road to Whitburn as well. It was only when Fulwell began to appear at the beginning of the 20th Century that the rather more pretentious term Sea Road appeared. The beach area around the Cat and Dog Stairs was 'the posh end', and that at the Sea Lane stretch was 'Tentland'.

Sea Lane

"With the very best wishes for a happy birthday. From L. D."

Before the building of the promenade there was a grassy bank with steps down to the sands. As well as the attractions of the beach there were also entertainments of various sorts on the banks. A particular favourite was a man with a peg leg who was known as Daredevil Peggy. He used to climb a giant ladder of about 80 feet, and then leap into a blazing tank below. Honestly!

The Promenade and Cannonball Rocks
Judging from the kiosk and the clothing style this probably dates to the 1950s. Early morning walkers are on the Low Promenade while the first of the sunbathers are already basking in the strong sunshine from the east. In theory anyhow ... That stretch of the 'prom' between the Cat and Dog Stairs and Roker Beach is also known locally as Bikini Atoll because of the scanty swimsuits and their constant promise of 'fall-out' when barely attached to the voluptuous female frames draped all over this stretch! The outcrop of rocks just below the promenade produced another popular spectacle in the 1950s in the form of a small opening at beach level which funnelled the incoming waves through a blow hole at the promenade surface.

Wouldn't You Like to Change Places
"Dear Mary, this is a glorious day and I am making the best of it at Seaburn. Cis." This is addressed to Miss M. Cummings, St. Chads, Cheetham Hill Road, Manchester.

New Promenade, looking North
"We expect to return on Saturday. Would you please get me a loaf of bread & some milk. We may be late. Train was slow. Very hot weather. Kindest regards. J.B." This is addressed to a Mrs. Thomas in Oswestry, Shropshire (possibly Francis Road). The promenade was built by the council in the 1930s. Some people would say that that was when the 'golden age' ended and that council regulation and control began to eliminate the individuality and character of the seafront.

On the Sands, Seaburn

The Promenade

The steps down to the promenade from Cliff Park at this point have long been known as the Cat and Dog Stairs and the reason for this name is very unclear. It appears that the original Cat and Dog Stairs led from the top of the Roker ravine in the park to beach level, emerging near the so-called Spottie's Hole. It is suggested that they were called thus because some of the steps were large - suitable for dogs, and some were small - suitable for cats (very refined!), or because pets used to be bathed in rock pools near that section of the promenade, or because dead dogs and cats were often thrown into the sea and the currents frequently brought the carcases into this bay! They all seem a little unlikely. This seems to be quite a recent view in fact, probably the 1970s. There is illumination equipment in place on Cliff Park.

The Beach, Sea Lane

Tentland, Seaburn
The message is addressed to Mrs. Horsham, 3 Ferguson Place, Burntisland, Fife, Scotland. It is dated 23 September, 1938. It is derived from what might be called the minimalist school of postcard writing.
"Hope to see you soon. Having a good time. E.G."

There were about ten different hirers of tents in a fiercely competitive business. The tents were put up for the users and they would obviously prefer the ones nearest the water. In the 1930s the tents came in three sizes and prices. The small ones were sixpence (in proper money ... 2.5 pence a day in present terminology), the medium sized tents were a shilling (5 pence) a day and the palatial were one shilling and sixpence (7.5 pence) per day. Stools could be had for twopence, deck chairs threepence and card tables for threepence. You had to pay a threepenny deposit for the tents. There were people who made an income for themselves by taking the tents back on behalf of the hirers and obtaining the deposit as payment. Of course if you couldn't afford a tent you had to cultivate the art of performing a striptease beneath a towel, which could occasionally go dramatically wrong. There were also people called 'sandscratchers' who made a living by finding money lost on the beach or items which could be sold.

Tentland, Seaburn

"Do you know this! I hope mammie got the parcel with the cake alright. Grannie is going up the river in the *Bullenfield* I think the name of the boat is. I hope Eileen walks with you now. Love from Grandpa and Grannie." This card is addressed to Miss Margaret Smith at Bradford Lodge, Alderley, Chelford, Cheshire. Presumably Eileen was a baby sister.

A postcard with exactly the same scene was also sent to Yorkshire.

"Roker, Sunderland. Mrs. Pearson. Just a card to say we arrived alright after a comfy journey. We are just fixing our tent up here today. Children all enjoying themselves ... Weather beautiful and fine. Love from all. Kisses from all. XXXX. E. Mills XX." The card is addressed to Mrs. Pearson, Thornhill, Sowood, Stainland, W. Halifax.

Tents were for hire from the Corporation from the 1930s. To get the best pitch for the day members of the family would get to the beach as early as possible to try and hold an area of sand to accommodate the family following behind, with dad carrying the tent. The strange tripod structure in the top left which looks like a drilling rig was a safety device used by the lifeguards. One end of a rope was fixed to it and the other end to a jetty or bathing platform so that the lifeguard could attach to the rope with a free running loop and be prevented from being swept away. The tents were usually uniformly coloured cream or green. This was a nightmare for small children struggling from the sea and trying to make their way back to their own tent while confronted with what must have seemed like a city. The evocatively named 'Lost Children Centre' up on the promenade was usually quite busy. Some people made their own tents.

Whitburn Bents.   Near Sunderland.

Whitburn Bents
Usually the views are along the beach at Whitburn The date is October

WHITBURN BENTS.

Whitburn Bents
"Am having fine sunny weather. Only cold in the wind. We generally sit facing this place called the Bent. Granny always likes to have the same seat & as it would not be kind to leave her by herself I have to sit with her. Hoping all are well. Rose Joicey" The card is addressed to Mrs. Wilson, 85 Violet Street, Benwell, Newcastle on Tyne. The date is not clear. The author has crossed out the original surname so she may have just been recently married (or divorced).

The Promenade, Seaburn

This is a modern card. It is dated 1961. It is addressed to Mr. S. Agate, 5 Northbrook Road, West Croydon, Surrey. The message reads "Dear Sid and Mike. Sorry I haven't written sooner, one day I forgot the cards, another the stamp, then we've been out a lot. Mother is keeping well, weather is good, but not much sun. Hope you are being a good boy Mike and not giving your Dad any worry. Won't be long now before I see you. Time is going very quick. Love from Ruth XX." This is from Mike's sister presumably. She sounds my kind of easily diverted postcard writer! Hopefully poor Mike got his card before Ruth got home.

Seaburn Hall

"We are Not Downhearted at Sunderland"
What can you say! Unfortunately nowadays this nice card might be seen as in poor taste by political correctness mind controllers. Sunderland, or rather Roker and Seaburn, continued to be a holiday destination until the 1950s. Then the combination of the spread of motor car ownership, the appearance of the overseas package holiday and rising incomes meant the decline of such traditional seaside resorts.

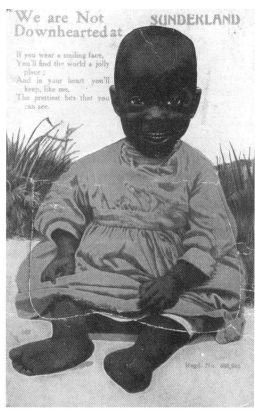

ME NO WANT TO LEAVE
SUNDERLAND

"Me no want to leave Sunderland."
What better can be said to conclude this tour and memories of the town?

FURTHER READING

As far as the history of Sunderland is concerned the most recent bibliographical information is to be found in Milburn, Geoffrey and Miller, Stuart (eds.) *Sunderland: River, Town and People*. However, your reading of this book may have also stimulated an interest in the tinted world of postcards and their senders. In that case you may wish to dip into one or more of the following:

Alderson, Frederick *The Comic Postcard in English Life* (David and Charles, 1970)
Byatt, Anthony *Picture Postcards and their Publishers* (Golden Age Postcard Books, 1978)
Carline, Richard *Pictures in the Post* (Gordon Fraser, 1971)
Hill, C.W. *Discovering Picture Postcards* (Shire, 1970)
Holt, Tonie and Holt, Valmai *Picture Postcards of the Golden Age* (MacGibbon and Kee, 1971)
Staff, Frank *The Picture Postcard and its Origins* (Lutterworth Press, 1966)

Magazines:
Picture Postcard Monthly
The British Postcard Collectors' Magazine